Advance Praise For
DIVERSITY BLUES

"Every leader needs *Diversity Blues*. It is an outstanding book. Whatever our race, we need to learn more about people of different backgrounds. We need to understand race and gender issues with full respect, for they make their impact on our lives, our families, communities, organizations, and our world. Our future depends on it!"
—Dorothy I. Height, Chair and President Emerita,
National Council of Negro Women, Inc.

"Amidst the vast literature about diversity comes Gladys Hankins' *Diversity Blues*, a brilliant dissection of how racism and sexism haunt the work place. Hankins unique contribution is to offer practical solutions to thorny problems that plague large and small organizations. This is a well conceived, clearly written and forcefully argued book that details how organizations can overcome bigotry to become viable institutions. *Diversity Blues* is a gold mine for the taking."
—Michael Eric Dyson, Ph.D., author of *I May Not Get There With You*, and professor at DePaul University

"*Diversity Blues* is a must read for all working men and women who are committed to eliminating prejudice and discrimination in the workplace. Dr. Hankins' book makes us more aware of racial and gender discrimination that exists, and offers solutions to help remedy these problems. Much of corporate success in the 21st Century will depend on how well we learn from the messages of *Diversity Blues*."
—William H. Gray, President, United Negro College Fund

"Sometimes you're on the road and the car in front of you is going too slow. 'Woman driver,' you mutter as you swing around and see that it is not a woman, but rather your own prejudice that made you ascribe to a cliché. *Diversity Blues* will help you put thoughts and assumptions into a clearer view. Dr. Hankins offers advice for both the business and the everyday world, helping all of us to understand how much better, how much more productive, how much more efficient life is when we open our hearts and minds."
—Nikki Giovanni, Poet

"Gladys Hankins has created a book that few could match. From her depth of real experience, she highlights issues that often the theorists miss. Further, she describes the needs, and outlines the solutions, with fairness and eloquence."

—Judith D. Palmer, Ph.D., Associate Director, Global IWS Education and Training, The Procter & Gamble Company

"*Diversity Blues* is an excellent book that represents an insider's unique view of workplace realities. Over time, there have been successes and missed opportunities to make diversity work in American organizations. *Diversity Blues* offers a roadmap to reach new heights in the New Millennium."

—Nathaniel R. Jones, Judge, U.S. Court of Appeals, Sixth Circuit

Make a difference!

Gladys Gossett Hankins, Ph.D.

DIVERSITY BLUES

DIVERSITY BLUES

How to Shake'em

Gladys Gossett Hankins, Ph.D.

With Foreword by Edwin L. Artzt, Former CEO
The Procter & Gamble Company

Telvic Press, Inc.
Cincinnati, Ohio

Publisher's Cataloging-in-Publication
(Provided by Quality Books, Inc.)

Hankins, Gladys Gossett.
    Diversity blues : how to shake'em / Gladys Gossett
  Hankins ; with foreword by Edwin L. Artzt -- 1st ed.
    p. cm.
    Includes bibliographical references and index.
    LCCN: 00-090719
    ISBN: 0-9679110-0-1

    1. Diversity in the workplace -- United States.
  2. Personnel management -- United States. 3. Pluralism
(Social sciences) -- United States. I. Title.

HF5549.5.M5H36 2000   658.3'008
                             QB100-700

First Edition 10 9 8 7 6 5 4 3
Printed in the United States of America

Cover designed by Emily Freeman

Published by Telvic Press, Inc.
Cincinnati, Ohio

Distributed by Seven Hills Book Distributors
Cincinnati, Ohio

ATTENTION: CORPORATIONS AND NON-PROFIT ORGANIZATIONS
This book is available at quantity discounts with bulk purchase for business or educational use. For information, contact Seven Hills Book Distributors, 1531 Tremont Street, Cincinnati, OH 45214, (513) 471-4300. Please provide quantity needed and a description of how the book will be used.

To the memory of my parents,
Anna Telora and Irving Victor Gossett,
and my aunt Gladys Hortense Cotton
who taught me that I could.

"Locality, nationality, race, sex, religion or social manner may differ, but the accord of desire for civil liberty is ever the same."

Mifflin Wistar Gibbs, Shadow and Light [1902]

CONTENTS

PART I IDENTIFYING THE PROBLEM

PART II Discussing the Issues

PART III SHAKING THE DIVERSITY BLUES

ACKNOWLEDGEMENTS

A number of friends and associates gave me critical feedback and a great deal of support and encouragement to pursue this project. I am ever grateful to them all. My sisters Martha Stafford, Joyce Clark, and Marjorie Jardan were a constant source of encouragement and helpful perspective, as were my friends, Joyce Morehead, Jarrow Merenivitch and S. Gene Washington.

The first person to read this book and share his views was Earnest Thompson. His enthusiasm greatly energized me to go forward with this work. Many others either read the book or in many ways were a continuing source of encouragement, insight and improvement ideas: Denise Andrews, Regina Smith, Joyce Lewis, Mary Lou Krohn, Lisa Gutierrez, Kimberly McClendon, Evelyn Ferguson, Martha White, Howard Elliott, Elmer Jackson, Richard Burns, Gary Simpson, Donna Shaw, Sylvie Vanvloodorp, Danielle Pion, Arlene Schecter, Cristina Chuecos, Heidi vanTriet and Dr. Judith Palmer.

A special appreciation to Shirley Serey who offered frank, valuable critique. Her input led to major refinements and improvements. Mary Anne Gale extended a vote of confidence by reading a section of this book to a seminar audience. I am extremely proud of the positive and overwhelming impact her reading had on that audience.

Cleo Gutierrez and Evelyn Davis both gave generously of their time to edit the book. The final editing was done by Dr. Nancy Spence who helped transform my manuscript into a succinct, crisp, to-the-point, and easy-to-follow book.

By writing the hard-hitting Foreword, Edwin L. Artzt, former CEO, The Procter & Gamble Company, added immeasurably to the credibility and relevancy of *Diversity Blues*. I am grateful for his contribution.

Finally, throughout the book, I quote a number of people with whom I have come in contact over the years. Their messages have been powerful and I wanted to share them. Thanks to everyone who offered their experiences so that others might learn.

FOREWORD

Edwin L. Artzt, Chairman and CEO
The Procter & Gamble Company
January 1990 - July 1995

Employees are our most important resource. As business leaders, we know it is smart to utilize the total contributions of all employees. In doing this, however, organizations face human-relations challenges.

Among these are racism and sexism. In spite of our best efforts to create wholesome work environments, these subtly entrenched conditions wreak havoc in our workplaces. In addition to the moral and ethical dilemmas they pose, racism and sexism have a negative impact on business success. Corporations determined to survive, grow, and compete must effectively combat them.

In 1995, on behalf of The Procter & Gamble Company, I accepted the Salute to Greatness Award by the King Center in Atlanta, Georgia. This award honors the life and works of Dr. Martin Luther King, Jr.

As it gave me opportunity to share my commitment to diversity, specifically, the necessity of organizational leaders to take a more proactive role in combatting racism, addressing this historic event was a unique privilege. While the subject of my comments was racism, I also feel as passionate about the need to attack problems of sexism.

Following are excerpts from that address:

> *"It's overwhelming to receive an award like this ... to stand alongside so many of you-—the King family, the Evers family, Dr. Height—people who have given so much and have paid so dearly for the cause of civil rights in this country.*
>
> *I can't compare my contribution to yours, but I share your conviction. And though I can never fully understand the pain of racism, I have seen the gain that can be achieved from true diversity in the workplace.*
>
> *And I deeply believe that as long as our society permits racism to limit the growth and contribution of talented people, we'll achieve only a fraction of our potential as individuals, as organizations, as a nation.*
>
> *Racism touches every aspect of our lives. It begins in our homes, where children hear things—and develop the fear and false sense of superiority that produce racist behavior in adults.*

That's why I believe so strongly that we must stop racism early—before it takes root—when people are very young. It's why P&G has supported programs like the Children's Campaign, led by the Leadership Conference Education Fund.... But we also have an obligation to the men and women who are being affected today by racism.

Five years ago, I was convinced that racism in the workplace was a structural problem—a problem that could be fixed like any other business challenge, with good strategies and clear accountability for success. I've learned since then that structural solutions aren't enough. They're important—we're making progress advancing women and minority men, and we've pretty much eliminated the most obvious blatant forms of racism in our organization because we've made it clear that overt racist behavior simply won't be tolerated.

But we've had much less success at eliminating the more subtle racism that lurks just under the surface—the kind that Marian Anderson described perfectly when she said, 'It's like hair across your cheek. You can't see it; you can't find it with your fingers; but you keep brushing at it, because the feel of it is irritating.' That kind of racism is as debilitating a force today as the ugly brutality of Albany and Birmingham and Selma a generation ago.

When I was here two years ago, I tried to describe my perception of this subtle, beneath-the-surface racism, and I think those words are just as valid today: I've come to realize that the most subtle forms of racism are sometimes the most destructive, especially in the workplace.

Young black managers I've talked with refer to it as the 'pain threshold'—the added burden that results from having one's opinions discounted, from failing to receive deserved credit or recognition, or having to work to a different standard than one's peers and seldom receiving the benefit of the doubt in close-call situations. Subtle, debilitating, largely unrecognized racism. We have to deal with this.

But dealing with this kind of racism is harder because it rarely shows its face. Nevertheless, as long as we find its tracks in our companies and in society at large, we must continue to fight it in every way we can.

One way we've done this at P&G is to conduct 'cultural audits' that help us unmask even the most subtle forms of racism... These audits, which have been conducted by objective outsiders like Roosevelt Thomas, are invaluable tools because they help us identify aspects of our culture *that can disguise and even perpetuate racist behavior. And they help us develop concrete action plans so we can address these issues head on— and we have.*

But I think the most important thing we do—the most important thing any of us can do—is to provide strong personal leadership at every level and especially from the top. To really make a lasting difference, senior managers like me have to roll up our sleeves and get involved in the process.

It's not enough to set numerical targets and challenge the organization to meet them. Instead, the most senior managers ... need to know their most promising minority managers—not as statistics, but as individuals.

If we want to make change happen, it's our responsibility to find out why those employees are not being advanced and to personally ensure that they get the development, the coaching and the opportunities they need to move up in the organization.

Without that kind of hands-on involvement by senior management, progress will always come slowly, if at all. But with it, we can create a management culture that will cascade from the top through every level of the organization.

I believe as deeply as I can that those of us who lead must set strong personal examples—not by merely encouraging diversity ... but by practicing it. Visibly. In our own lives. That's the real obligation of leadership, and it's an obligation that I pledge to fulfill as I accept this award."

Preparing my speech required having insightful discussions with individuals with whom I had not talked these issues before. I realized that senior managers, often far removed from the majority of the workforce, should seek out more opportunities to discuss pertinent issues with members of other racial, ethnic, and gender groups. What we learn may often surprise us.

My message to the King Center was delivered to an audience committed to eradicating prejudice and discrimination. I now want to offer corporate leaders a message that applies to sexism just as it does to racism.

Start by acknowledging the existence of problems. Mere acknowledgment will begin to drive you, as it did me, to take a more aggressive stand against prejudice and discrimination in your organizations.

Through a clear, concise, and insightful message, Dr. Hankins makes a compelling case for tackling these problems. While the process may be very difficult, the end result is that everyone in the organization, and the organization itself, stands to gain.

Dr. Hankins' persistent involvement has been instrumental in contributing to the progress we have made at Procter & Gamble. I am very clear, however, that, in spite of progress already made, there is still much left to do. I say this with a conviction amassed from more than 40 years in corporate management.

Corporate leaders, read and take note. Then act.

Edwin L. Artzt, Former Chairman and CEO
The Procter & Gamble Company

PREFACE

All across American organizations, conversations about human differences are taking place. But the subject of diversity seems to bring out the pessimist in everyone. Witness the following:

SCENE I:

Two black women lunching in the dining room of a typical U.S. company.

Black Woman #One: *You won't believe this. Today during my performance appraisal, I was told my output was good, but I needed to work on my attitude.*

Black Woman #Two: *I had practically the same experience. In fact, my boss informed me that I need to smile more because people are reluctant to approach me. Marsha, I am so tired of this.*

Black Woman #One: *I don't think there's a black person alive whose style hasn't been critiqued. They want us to be just like them; otherwise, we're not okay.*

Black Woman #Two: *Then I guess I'll never be okay by their standards.*

SCENE II:

Two white men playing golf at an exclusive golf course.

White Man #One: *Say, Don, did I tell you about our next big project? We're going to need someone to take the lead. Success on this would mean a sure path to vice president. Interested?*

White Man #Two: *Sure am. But what about affirmative action? Don't you think they'll want to put another woman or minority in the position? They even gave that Eastern-Division sales job to a woman.*

Anymore, those people seem to get all the best jobs.

White Man #One: *Don't you worry about a thing. I'll take care of that.*

SCENE III:

Conference room of a major corporation. Two white women are the first to arrive at an important meeting.

White Woman #One: *Look at you, Carol! In that outfit, you could pass for "one of the guys."*

White Woman #Two: *I figure as long as I dress like they do, I won't stand out as much and they'll take me more seriously. But frankly, I hate this suit.*

White Woman #One: *I know what you mean. Why do we do this to ourselves just to try to be successful on the job?*

SCENE IV:

The hallways of corporate America. Two black men walking toward each other.

Black Man #One: *Say, Guy, where are you hurrying off to?*

Black Man #Two: *George wants to see me right away. He's going to tell me again what's wrong with my report. I thought I had nailed it this time. It's like he just has to find something wrong with it. I'll be here all night again working on it.*

Black Man #One: *Hey, don't waste your time. You know and I know, it will probably never be "good enough." Besides, I bet your work is twice as good as Ed's, your white counterpart. But he's George's boy.*

Black Man #Two: *Don't I know it. He'll probably be getting promoted any day now.*

Black Man #One: *I rest my case!*

Thousands of similarly negative conversations or thoughts occur daily. Despite the many years corporations have been addressing race and gender issues, nearly everyone is still "crying the blues." Some things have just not changed that much.

ABOUT THIS BOOK

Diversity Blues discusses diversity primarily in the context of its two most devastating problems—prejudice and discrimination. Prejudice is simply *adverse judgment without examining the facts,* and discrimination is *behavior marked by prejudice.* These problems show up in organizations in varied ways, including as racism and sexism.

Diversity Blues helps readers identify the problem—an important first step since many people today are not really convinced there is one. Furthermore, it proposes dealing directly with the root causes, not simply the symptoms. It explores beliefs, stereotypes, and racial/gender issues. And as a means to achieving full diversity, it champions the use of principles to deal with human differences instead of only laws.

I was asked why I would write a book about a topic that most people feel is passé. *"Don't you know people don't want to read about this issue anymore? Things are different now and people are tired of being reminded of the ways things used to be."* To those who share this view, here is the reality. In the 21st Century, things are different, it is true, but only in the ways prejudice and discrimination are acted out.

People prefer to not face or believe this ugly truth. Therefore, many have learned to cover it up quite masterfully. The more layers put on it, the less people are reminded that it exists. Like a nasty sore that is covered with soothing salve and layers of bandages but never heals until it is exposed to air, that is the way it is with the issues that will be discussed in this book. We will carefully, but firmly, remove the bandages. Having done this, the reader will be able to clearly see the problem, acknowledge it, and it is expected, be moved to remedy it.

The reader should know that the subject of prejudice and the many forms of discrimination that result from it are not pretty. Attempts to soften the discussion or rationalize the issues to make them more palatable will only serve to neutralize the message to the point that it has little or no effect, at least none that would move people to action.

Specifically, this book challenges patterns of thinking and behavior that have long served to provide some people with certain benefits at the expense of others. It demonstrates that prejudice and discrimination negatively affect employee morale as well as over-all organizational effectiveness. It shows how constructive diversity management results in long-term improvement in productivity, effectiveness, and profitability, transforming workplaces into consummately healthy and productive environments.

One chapter investigates what white men face as they are compelled to deal with changes brought on by workforce diversity. Another is dedicated to the role that women of all races and minority men play in bringing about change—individually, in groups, and in partnership with white men.

Final chapters provide answers to the much-asked question: *"Where do we go from here?"* (Leaders usually ask this when they finally realize the seriousness of the issues and want concrete strategies to bring about improvement in employee utilization, retention, morale, productivity, and relationships.)

Most of the data for this book comes from personal communications, observations, and experiences during my more than twenty-five years in management in a major American corporation. I also acquired numerous insights from over twenty years of developing and facilitating cultural-diversity workshops and programs for hundreds of people in organizations across the U.S. and internationally.

Many words from these workshops, meetings, and private discussions were communicated so powerfully and movingly that it always seemed unfortunate that a larger audience did not have a chance to learn from them. Therefore, I have incorporated a number of the most poignant and memorable. They are special teachable moments, and through this book, the reader will be invited to share them. I have attempted to convey the full spirit, intent, and impact with which they were originally delivered.

Because words spoken in workshops and private conversations are confidential, neither speakers nor their corporations will be named. However, prejudice and discrimination are not linked to geography nor limited to a particular industry or socio-economic level. They can occur in almost any organization and within almost any group.

It has been observed that people tend to have positive reactions to diversity discussions when presented in a straightforward manner—not sugarcoated or glossed over. Because this style has proven time and again to be extremely effective, it will be the approach used in this book.

Many people believe the goal of diversity awareness is to understand other people's differences. However, it is important to note that understanding why people are as they are is not a prerequisite for healthy interactions and relationships. The problems addressed in this book are ones that occur when certain physiological differences are believed to represent deficiencies and treated accordingly, while others are prized and accorded privileged status.

The intent of this book, therefore, is not necessarily for readers to understand all human differences. Rather it is for them to learn why they have come to believe as they do about people who exhibit certain differences, and to understand the impact of their beliefs on their attitudes and behaviors. Once they have this self-awareness, they can decide whether or not to make a change.

WHO SHOULD READ THIS BOOK

First, *Diversity Blues* will help every female and minority-male reader understand, articulate, and deal constructively with the issues they face in organizations. If it does nothing else, it will show them that the sexism and racism they face are real, not figments of an overly sensitive imagination. They will gain strength from discovering that they are not alone, and insight into strategies to change things from an empowered position.

Second, the book will serve as a resource for organization leaders who wish to create a more productive work environment by making fuller use of their diverse work forces and eliminating those interpersonal elements that distract from their effectiveness.

Additionally, the book is for anyone who desires to better understand diversity issues and what they can do to address them.

Although the principle beneficiaries from the removal of hostile attitudes and stereotypes are the people most directly targeted by them, ultimately everyone stands to benefit from their elimination. For surely, the lives of non-targeted others are enriched by the release of these negative and onerous thought processes.

Finally, many in organizations have been content with simply meeting the legislative intent of civil-rights laws while choosing not to tackle employee attitudes, beliefs, and values. But attitudes, beliefs, and values are inextricably tied to employee fulfillment, job satisfaction, job productivity, and ultimately, organizational success. It is time to tackle them. It is time to shake off those diversity blues.

Gladys Gossett Hankins, Ph.D.

PART 1
Identifying the Problem

☆ THE NEED FOR EFFECTIVELY MANAGED DIVERSITY

☆ ISSUES IN DIVERSITY

☆ PREJUDICE AND DISCRIMINATION— DO THEY REALLY EXIST?

"One problem thoroughly understood is of more value than a score poorly mastered."

Booker Taliaferro Washington
Address to the Alabama State Teacher's Association,
Montgomery, Alabama (April 11, 1888)

ONE

THE NEED FOR EFFECTIVELY MANAGED DIVERSITY

Prejudice and discrimination are deterrents to productive, healthy organizations and must be sought out and driven from the organization.

Since waste of any kind can be costly, organizations must utilize all resources effectively. However, unlike resources that are quantifiable, measurable, and predictable, human resources are tougher to manage because human behavior is not entirely predictable. Humans can perform differently under what may appear to be the same circumstances. Compounded by the entrance of prejudice and discrimination, although not always readily visible, these variables can have an extremely negative effect on human resources. Can organizations afford that?

EFFECTIVELY MANAGING DIVERSITY

Employee contributions can be maximized when people operate in a non-hostile, supportive environment free of prejudice and discrimination. Certainly, those directly affected by a discriminatory environment must appropriate work time and mental energies to issues associated with real or perceived prejudice and discrimination. Some people estimate spending as much as 30 percent or more of their work time dealing with such issues, thereby reducing the time they have for business. Sometimes the stress of such issues lingers long after the matter has ended—with detrimental effects on productivity.

Another factor: as opportunities increase for women and minority men, the voices of unhappy white men are surfacing in ever-increasing numbers. A possibility not often considered is that some loss of productivity occurs as white men learn to deal with, or reject, organizational diversity efforts. In addition, affected individuals may prematurely separate from the organization—at a significant cost to the establishment, not just to the women or minority men who leave.

Then, there are the external influences. The possibility of lawsuits, compounded by loss of goodwill, public trust and potential customers prompted one corporate manager to remark, *"The cost of doing the right thing can be much less than the cost of doing the wrong thing."*

Given the dynamic nature of human relations, leaders should know there is a definite connection between prejudice, its counterpart, discrimination, and reduced employee productivity. The specific relationship between dollar losses and poor human-resources management may not be readily calculable or apparent. What is certain is that any unproductive use of labor diminishes an organization's ability to function optimally.

Over time, such losses may show up as higher recruiting expenses, turnover and absences, poor-quality output, health and safety issues, lowered employee performance and diminished organizational productivity. These losses are further compounded as they become entrenched in daily operations, ending up as organizational norms. It should not be too difficult to understand how organizations ultimately suffer.

To all this, the successful businessperson could respond, *"But, our organization is already doing quite well. Why change anything?"* Obviously, change must clearly be justifiable before an organization undertakes it, so this reaction is natural and logical. Yet, leaders need only ask whether it would matter if all their employees functioned consistently at peak levels. As many employees in today's corporations are being underutilized, even in the most successful organizations, consistent, across-the-board, peak employee performance would make a huge difference. Thus, any effort that increases individual contributions leads to greater organizational success.

The annual productivity increase in the United States is around three percent a year. Today, some nations are exceeding that rate.

For example, in Japan, the productivity-improvement rate in recent years has been twice as high (Walanabe, 1991). If other countries can accomplish such results, why can the U.S. not do the same? What is happening inside American corporations that causes them to produce less than optimally?

For one thing, the U.S. work force has a more diverse makeup than many countries. Could the way our corporations deal with their diverse human resources have something to do with this? Very possibly, for while diversity has the potential to be an advantage, if managed poorly, it can be a disadvantage.

If America is to retain its position as the number one economic power, it can ill afford to lag behind its international competitors, especially in the critical area of work force productivity. Top management must realize that ongoing problems in managing a race-and-gender-diverse work force are bound to have a negative effect on the bottom line, even more so if problems are not handled well.

Work force projections as we enter the 21st Century suggest that the imperative to manage diversity effectively is only going to increase. Three minority groups (African-Americans, Asians, and Hispanics) are projected to comprise more than 25 percent of the population, and 29 percent of work force entrants (Martin & Ross-Gordon, 1990). American-born white men will drop from 46 percent in the mid 1990's to around 39 percent of the work force. U.S.-born white women will enter the work force at a rate three times that of white men (Abbasi & Hollman, 1991).

Even for organizations now making satisfactory progress, the work force represented by these projections obviously presents challenges. Maintaining the standard of living in the U.S. that millions have come to take for granted will require the effective incorporation of female- and minority-male work force entrants with minimal disruption or loss of productivity. The responsibility and accountability for this clearly rests on the shoulders of top management.

MANAGING DIVERSITY

Not everyone understands what managing diversity entails. For example, a white-male, Ivy-League college student said, *"We're certainly much in favor of ethnic and racial diversity at this college... which has been attained."* To this student, managing diversity meant only having a diverse enrollment.

Leaders sometimes assume they manage diversity effectively when they offer diversity training, plan for affirmative-action, accommodate employees with disabilities or post equal-employment notices on company bulletin boards. Others create and staff diversity positions, establish special mentoring programs, and offer seminars on career management to women and minority men (Livingston, 1991). If activities like these constitute an organization's total efforts, it is being reactive rather than proactive, thus, limiting its potential progress. The effective management of diversity involves much more than these steps.

Diversity management is an *ongoing* process, not just a program or series of activities. As such, it must be built into every facet of the business, and basic human-relations principles for dealing with individual differences adhered to by, and applied to all people. As managing diversity moves beyond legal compliance to addressing the human attitudes and behaviors that first created the need for laws, the spirit of managing human differences is at work.

Speaking of the failure of leaders to truly appreciate the complexities of human attitudes and behaviors, Peggy McIntosh (1986) referred to a state board of regents voting to prohibit racism in its higher-education system. *"It is not possible to simply prohibit racism the way you can prohibit smoking,"* she explains. *"How do we go about thinking about and working to change understanding of what racism is to the point where no one thinks you can simply prohibit it?"*

When diversity is managed proactively, the organization eliminates discrepancies based on racial, gender, or cultural differences. It ceases recruitment, termination, training, development, placement, disciplinary action, promotional, and salary practices that advantage some groups while disadvantaging others.

In one study of a number of Fortune 500 companies, some were being touted for effectively managing diversity even as they were making little progress in key non-visible areas. Leaders who believe their companies are doing well managing diversity should see an equitable distribution of all groups of employees across all levels and functions of their organizations. They should ask: do *all* our employees work in a non-hostile atmosphere? Do they feel valued? Do any feel discriminated against for reasons of race or gender?

Many organizational leaders recognize that racial and gender diversity is important. Yet few, if any, have insisted on achieving parity across all employee groups, and fewer can claim to have ended the prejudicial attitudes that produced discriminatory practices. These practices will not go away unaided, and as long as they exist in organizations, so too, will associated problems. There is much room for improvement.

In no other area have organizations settled for such limited progress as that made in managing diversity. Through resourcefulness, innovation, technical mastery, commitment, creativity, and sheer determination, American businesses have repeatedly shown that they usually accomplish whatever they decide to go after. Why then are we not getting better results in managing diversity? Perhaps the answer is that American businesses usually accomplish *whatever they decide to go after.*

LEGISLATION-BASED DIVERSITY MANAGEMENT

Legislation can be credited with compelling organizations to alter employment practices, thus opening the doors of opportunity to other groups, particularly in non-traditional roles. Such legislation included the Civil Rights Act of 1964 prohibiting discrimination based on (among other things) race and gender, and Executive

Order 11246 requiring organizations to develop affirmative-action plans to address the disparities caused by decades of segregation and discrimination. Other governmental interventions preceded these laws, and still others have followed.

However, a multitude of problems accompanied the changing work force brought about by this legislation. For example, many people had difficulty adjusting to bosses who were not white males. Or, at times, women or minority men were placed in positions where they failed because they lacked the requisite training, skills, and capabilities. Often white men failed to understand or welcome the intrusion of women and minority men into their formerly closed circles.

Yet, in spite of the challenges, there have been notable successes. Many women and minority men attribute to equal-employment legislation their placement into formerly white-male roles. A few have risen to key executive levels. Certainly, numerous changes have been made because of such legislation.

Yet, this legislation has come under attack for failing to bring about positive, lasting change. Perpetuating popular myths, opponents of civil-rights-driven hiring practices have described them as the lowering of standards to accommodate *less-qualified* people, as *reverse discrimination*. Legislation has also been criticized for failure to generate commitment from organizational leaders who merely complied with minimum requirements, rather than the spirit, of law.

Quota systems, often associated with affirmative-action programs, have also been unpopular among white men as well as women and minority men. White men say it is wrong to set aside positions based on race or gender. As organizations *play the numbers game*, women and minority men say there is limited access to upper levels to all but a *predetermined* few.

In many cases, what some have viewed as progress, others have seen as regression, and problems associated with racial, gender, and other differences in the workplace continue to negatively affect business results in important areas like costs, productivity, and use of resources (Cox and Blake, 1991).

It has become painfully clear that civil-rights laws are not enough. This critical legislation provided the initial impetus to change hiring and workplace practices, but legislation alone cannot cause organizational members to *accept or embrace* these changes. Full diversity requires a move from a legislative to a principle-based approach to diversity management.

PRINCIPLE-BASED DIVERSITY MANAGEMENT

Principle-based diversity management facilitates environments in which their members are free to contribute fully to organizational success. To guide diversity practices, leaders may either develop their own principles (codes of conduct to influence how people think and act) or they may apply the basic common-sense canons for healthy, productive relationships identified below.

Principles For Treating Human Differences:

- All organizational personnel deserve to be treated with respect and dignity.
- Individual differences can be visible and invisible. Addressing invisible differences is as important as addressing visible ones.
- People should treat each other fairly and equitably.
- Talent, intelligence, skills, and abilities are distributed among all groups.
- No one should be advantaged or disadvantaged relative to others by virtue of his or her membership in a particular group.
- Prejudice and discrimination are deterrents to productive, healthy organizations and must be sought out and driven from the organization.
- People should be treated as individuals—not just as members of a group.

- It is not appropriate to prejudge, stereotype or discriminate against others for reasons that include race, gender, ethnicity, age, religion, or physical condition.

- Prejudice and discrimination are problems. Every person, by his or her attitudes or behavior, is either part of the solution or part of the problem.

- If people have the right information, and believe it to be true, they will generally be moved to action.

- All diversity issues should be addressed, including those pertaining to women, minority men and white men.

- All organizational members have a responsibility to help create the cultures in which they wish to work.

- It should be assumed that all employees want to succeed and are capable of doing so, and treated accordingly.

- A full appreciation for human diversity can be reached when people no longer define (or judge) each other based on cultural or physical attributes, but on the content of their charracter.

Principles are the cornerstones of organizational operations. All organizational members must unconditionally embrace them lest they become meaningless rhetoric. Organizations that manage diversity, not by laws, but by principles, open doors to greater success and profitability.

To remind readers that the thread throughout this book is principle-based diversity management, one of these principles will begin each chapter.

CONCLUSION

It is not very difficult to make a case for the effective management of diversity. Business success and survival may very well depend on it. Diversity management is an ongoing process, not just a program or series of activities. What is difficult is the successful implementation of this process.

Equal-employment laws will produce only limited change. When governmental legislation outlawed certain acts of discrimination, it did not end them. In many cases, it merely caused perpetrators to devise more sophisticated methods of carrying them out.

If human-diversity problems are to be permanently resolved, the cultures of organizations must be defined by a principle-based treatment of all people.

"The realization of ignorance
is the first act of knowing."

Jean Toomer, Definitions and Apherisms, LV (1931)

·Two·

ISSUES IN DIVERSITY

People should treat each other fairly and equitably.

The problem is well outlined statistically.... The problem is discrimination. The problem is prejudice* (King, 1981). Many in corporate America believe that because work force numbers for women of all races and minority men have increased, we have accomplished what we set out to do. A senior manager remarked, *"We no longer need quotas or special programs since now there are laws to protect people from discrimination. Diversity is here. Now we can get back to business."*

Another corporate manager stated, *"We've been doing diversity for a long time now. We're in pretty good shape with this diversity thing. We're well on our way to having the problem solved."*

The bottom-line reality is that, in spite of all the plaudits, we have not yet achieved full diversity in a prejudice and discrimination-free work environment. It stands to reason that social problems stemming from societal norms and practices also exist in our workplaces. Unfortunately, organizations enable these conditions to continue thriving, and as long as that is the case, a diverse work force cannot operate optimally.

It is true that there have been changes. However, in many cases, what was once blatant discrimination has been replaced by covert, subtle acts, making it even more devastating than before. Therefore, what remains to be achieved is the identification and elimination of these undesirable conditions. When accomplished, organizations will move from diversity typified by hostile, non-optimal work environments, to achieving full diversity—the harmonious, productive blending of diverse human types.

As the King quote above suggests, problems of discrimination and prejudice have cut a wide swath across U.S. workplaces. Racism and sexism are at the core.

Of course, race and gender do not constitute the total spectrum of diversity, which also includes ethnicity, religion, class, sexual orientation and many other differences, including invisible ones. However, in an increasingly multi-cultural work force where organizations are incorporating diverse members into positions previously held only by white males, probably every person will come in contact with racism and sexism, usually with unpleasant consequences.

Racism and Sexism

Since the enactment of Title VII of the Civil Rights Act and legislation requiring organizations to put in place affirmative action plans, there has been upheaval, backlash and disruption. In some cases, this upheaval takes the form of emotional employee protests such as, *"I'll never work for a woman or "I'll never let some n——- tell me what to do."* At times, managers who, themselves, may yearn for the good old days when government did not tell them how to run their businesses, meet such sentiments with open sympathy.

While some progress has been made, racism and sexism remain two of the tougher challenges organizations face as they move into the global 21st Century. Heavily taxing resources, they are issues no sound business can afford to ignore. Working to abolish prejudice and discrimination in organizations is plain and simply, a smart business strategy.

Institutional Racism and Sexism

Institutional racism and sexism can be defined as the ongoing, systematic mistreatment of women of all races and minority men in organizations. This treatment is solidly ingrained in workplace environments, covering an entire gamut of organizational elements— human systems, organizational structure, and business practices, policies, values, goals, principles, etc. If racism and sexism in organizations are to be eliminated, these organizational elements must be changed.

More than 20 years ago, Gibbs and Terry (1977) described racism and sexism as conditions existing ...

> *"when one race or sex group, intentionally or unintentionally, inequitably distributes resources; refuses to share power; maintains closed, unresponsive and inflexible policies, practices and programs; and imposes ethnocentric and gender-centric culture on another race or sex group for its supposed benefits. These actions are justified by blaming the other race or sex group."*

Dovido and Gaertner (1986, p.3) define the institutionalization of these conditions as *"the intentional or unintentional manipulation or toleration of institutional policies that unfairly restrict the opportunities of particular groups of people."* These policies can be written or unwritten and carried out by any member of the organization.

The primary benefit of eradicating or de-institutionalizing racism and sexism is that organizations gain a tremendous human resources opportunity—that of creating work environments that allow all employees to contribute at their fullest.

Unfortunately, there has been little sustained progress in creating prejudice and discrimination-free work environments. Today, women of all races and minority men say they still see and experience prejudice and discrimination. Reflecting at retirement on his more than 30 years in a major corporation, one African-American man had the following to say:

> *It is unfashionable to remind people that the fight is still going on and we are still very far from achieving the dream. The stereotypes of African Americans who try to achieve beyond what is viewed as acceptable is often that they are militant, hostile, uppity. We would like to believe these attitudes are no longer in place, but reality indicates otherwise...*
>
> *Some people say we are further separating ourselves by addressing these inequities. But we must continue to fight the inequities, even though the system claims they do not exist...*

During my formative years, we were told things would be better when we grew up. Instead, we have reverted to the "last-hired, first-fired" policy of my father's day. Today we are still judged more by the color of our skin than by the content of our character. If anyone thinks this does not exist anymore, he should open his eyes and look around. It's everywhere.

Race and gender-related problems persist, and some people feel they have actually gotten worse. One example that might support this: a typical U.S. corporation that began hiring women into management positions more than 25 years ago had little to show for its efforts by the late 1990's. Although this corporation had an impressive number of women managers, a closer examination showed their average length of service was between one and two years. Analyzed individually, a few women were found to have three or four years of service; the most senior woman had only a few more. Many had only months.

Considering that this company had actively recruited and hired women each year since it first began placing them in management positions more than two decades earlier, the question is, where did the others go? Obviously, for a number of reasons, they left the organization. For the record, some departures were voluntary, others, involuntary. Reasons varied. Many who voluntarily left said they were doing so to stay home with the family or to pursue other job opportunities.

Across America, women and minority men have higher turnover rates than white men. In some cases, their rate of attrition has been many times the rate of white men. According to Morrison (1993), this is likely due to limited career opportunities, disparity in pay and assignments, insufficient recognition, poor performance ratings, and few promotions. Several of the women and minority men who leave state that their number-one reason is an inability to progress up the ladder (Allen, 1991). If all things were equal and there were no prejudice and discrimination in organizations, the rate of separation should be about the same for white men, women of all races, and minority men.

Hitting an upper limit of mobility has been termed *the glass ceiling.* A survey conducted by the American Management Association substantiates its existence. Three-quarters of larger companies surveyed (those having 500 or more employees) responded that minorities at their firms were routinely overlooked for vital promotions (Management Review, 1993).

Although this survey specifically addressed minorities, the disproportionately small numbers of women in higher positions in larger corporations indicates that women of all races, like minority men, have also been routinely overlooked. Although white women have had limited movement, African-American and other-race women have had much less. A look at Fortune 2000 industrial and service companies found that only five percent of senior managers were women; virtually all were white (Federal Glass Ceiling Commission, March, 1995).

A key factor in de-institutionalizing racism and sexism is management accountability. Such accountability has been relatively non-existent. Remember, we are not too far removed from a time when overt acts of discrimination were sanctioned by custom and tradition. Indeed, studies show that leaders who actively support diversity risk a loss of prestige and credibility.

Because of his organization's chilly climate regarding women's issues, one high-level corporate manager sponsored a women's support network but chose to keep his sponsorship confidential. Regrettably, given the lack of acceptance in many workplaces for diversity initiatives, it is almost understandable why some managers do not openly challenge injustices.

In many organizations, rewards and recognition go to people whose efforts affect bottom-line profit, not to those who get involved in unpopular social issues, as managing cultural diversity has sometimes been called. A Department of Labor study of the glass ceiling found, in general, no negative consequences to managers who failed to support diversity programs (Snyder, 1993) *although there may have been repercussions to those who did.*

Since the advent of civil-rights legislation, organizational approaches to managing diversity have produced mostly short-term results. It is increasingly clear that the time has come to step up the effort.

WHY FOCUS ON WOMEN AND MINORITY MEN?

Here's a question many of you are probably wondering: since there are so many differences among people, why focus primarily on women and minority men? Because, both in scope and complexity, racial and gender differences tend to eclipse many other types of differences. Furthermore, as much as we might prefer to believe that racism and sexism have been resolved, they have not. Beliefs about race and gender are deeply imbedded, and tackling them is a huge challenge.

Many people do not know how to deal with differences. Perceptions of others are sometimes based purely on stereotypes: Asians are technically superior; Hispanics are not ambitious, etc. When participants in one workshop described their attitudes toward other cultural groups, responses ran the gamut from professions of tolerance *(live and let live)*; to fondness *(Some of my best friends are____)*; to intense dislike, hatred, jealousy, disdain, or anger.

From these responses, it can fairly be reasoned that certain groups are going to be subjected to discrimination. Even if people want their prejudices to remain private, they *will* surface. Consider the following comment of a white-male manager: *"Sounds like there's a nigger in the woodpile."* He made this remark speaking on the phone with a black female employee about a business matter. When he realized what he had said and to whom he was speaking, he tried to recover, but he failed to relieve her shock.

The woman reported the incident to her manager who immediately admonished the man. Unfortunately, this man's slip of the tongue created an uncomfortable, hostile environment for her.

I didn't know what to say to him. I had never heard this expression, "nigger in the woodpile," and frankly, I didn't have any idea what the phrase meant. I knew, of course, that it was derogatory because of the "N" word. Someone has since explained the meaning of the expression, and, yes, it is very derogatory and stereotypical.

I don't know if I believe this man was intentionally trying to insult me. It may have just slipped out. But that's the problem! You see, it had to come from somewhere in his mind. I figured this man probably had a problem with black people, and I could only assume that was how he felt about me too.

As you can imagine, dealing with him became very uncomfortable. And in my job I had to talk to him almost every day! It even affected my interactions with other white people at work, as I was always on the defensive, assuming that they felt the same way as this man did.

Was this an isolated incident? African Americans cite instance after instance of such behavior in U.S. workplaces.

Women tell similar stories. In the following, a white woman manager tells how a male colleague undermined her:

My manager was leading a meeting but had to leave before it was over. There were three or four items still to be covered in the meeting, so he asked me to handle the rest of the meeting.

I handled one item, and then called on a male colleague to present his topic. He took the floor all right, and he never sat down. When he was finished with his item, he called for the next topic, and the next. Finally, this man wrapped up the meeting! I never had the floor again.

It was like he just could not deal with me being in charge. I frankly did not quite know how to handle it, especially in the presence of all my colleagues... I stewed about the incident for a long time and wondered how I should have handled it.

One after another, women cite the slights and indignities they experience in the workplace, particularly if they happen to be the lone woman in a group. For example, every time one woman spoke up in a committee meeting, the leader would look at his watch and sigh as if exasperated that, once again, she was taking up their precious time. A frequent occurrence has been a woman's comments or suggestions in meetings later being ascribed to a man in the group.

The victims of such incidents are expected, even encouraged, to put them aside and function as if nothing had happened. *"You will want to be careful talking about sexism here,"* a white-male manager told a female subordinate manager who wanted to discuss being ignored by a speaker during a presentation to a large, predominately male group.

In spite of this woman raising her hand high, the speaker called on men all around her. As this continued, colleagues close by began to squirm in their seats, obviously becoming uncomfortable over what was happening. A man seated behind her pointed vigorously at her, thinking the speaker did not see her. Even still, the speaker failed to acknowledge her—and never called on her.

Several people later came up to ask her, *"What was the matter with that guy? Why did he keep ignoring you?"* The woman was unable to explain. She later described her reaction.

> *I wondered what was going on? Was I invisible or crazy? I felt hurt and angry being ignored, and I was especially embarrassed that so many of my co-workers had witnessed this.*
>
> *When I told my manager about it, he cautioned against bringing this matter up, telling me I might get "labeled."*
>
> *I was wiped out and upset. I can honestly say I couldn't function for the rest of the day, and it was a while before I got over this incident. I'm afraid I was quite hesitant about raising my hand for a long time after that.*

Women and minority men operate daily in environments filled with such incidents. The reason this may come as a surprise to many is that these behaviors are often visible only to women and minority men. After a lifetime of such experiences, they become quite adept at identifying and facing them—and keeping quiet about them in order to not be considered trouble makers.

Another reason this may suprise others is because, for the most part, women and minority men seem so normal, well adjusted and happy. Surely, if things were all that bad, it would devastate them, wouldn't it? Coping strategies will be discussed in a later chapter. Obviously, appearing happy is one of them.

Racism and sexism must be confronted head-on. Possibly because this is such a formidable challenge, managers have postponed facing them. Permeating every facet of organizations, cultural-diversity issues were said to be the biggest human-resources challenge of the 20th Century (Griggs and Louw, Eds., 1995).

Granted, it would be much easier for leaders to throw up their hands, admit powerlessness, and leave these tough issues to work themselves out. However, as long as women and minority men are treated differently in organizations, such reaction will offer only a temporary reprieve.

Organizations stand to benefit from tackling tough issues. Considering the growing numbers of women and minority men in the work force, the benefits of undertaking this agenda could be widespread, affecting all employees and total organizations.

Futhermore, unless we drastically change our ways, problems of race and gender will affect inter-cultural and international relations, too. Says one high-ranking corporate manager:

> We really don't have a clue about global differences. We are usually so busy judging or interpreting people from other countries that we don't place any real value on their cultural differences.

As Americans, we hold to our view that anyone who is not "one of us" is automatically not as good as we are. We think we are complimenting others when we tell them that we accept them as 'one of us,' a message that I have learned comes across as very condescending.

If we are going to play in the world market, we will have to learn to respect others for their differences.

THE AFRICAN AMERICAN DILEMMA

No racial or ethnic group in America—African American and other blacks, Asian/Asian American, Native American, Latin/Latin American, European American and others—has been completely free from stereotyping and bigotry. Certainly, in seeking to assimilate into the American melting pot, all groups have experienced discrimination, segregation, living with others' misperceptions, feeling the need to be twice as good while being treated as not as good, being in the spotlight (while sometimes feeling invisible), and having to deny their cultural heritage.

African Americans and Asian Americans (and, to some extent, certain other groups) experience further discrimination. Because of skin color, they never assimilate totally into white culture—not that they necessarily desire to. One Chinese-American did not find consoling the words, *"Don't worry, you are just like one of us."*

"I'm not white," he wanted to respond. *"My skin color is different from yours. I am different from you. I have my own culture and I want it to be recognized."*

The prevalent stereotype of Asians as *technical coolie* has made them highly sought after as the ideal minority. Unfortunately, they often enter American organizations to find themselves the only one of their culture or race.

An Asian American addressed the problem this way:

Asians and Hispanics do not have a Martin Luther King. If we did, we could be organized and companies might then be more compelled to address our concerns as they have begun to address the concerns of groups who are fortunate to have a critical mass, such as African Americans and even gays and lesbians.

I have worked in this company for 20 years. I started out as the only one, and I remain one of only a handful of Asians in my organization.

While recognizing that other ethnic groups experience prejudice and discrimination, the majority of examples I share will pertain largely to the black/white experience. This is because the racial experience about which I can speak most knowledgeably, both from rich personal and career experience, is that of African Americans. Importantly, however, insights and recommendations from the black/white discussion in this book can be transferable to other groups.

The history of blacks in America is unique. The effects of enslavement live on in every African American just as prejudice against black people and a belief in their inferiority live on in many whites. The extent to which slavery has affected black people over time has been debated, but it is clear that slavery's residuals are still evident and operational (York, 1994). Decades after the Emancipation Proclamation, black people are still routinely subjected to prejudice and discrimination.

Dr. Charles King, noted civil-rights advocate, once asked everyone in a group of white and black participants at his workshop if he or she was prejudiced. Each person answered in the affirmative. When they answered why they were prejudiced, blacks all said it was essentially a reaction to being discriminated against. To a person, whites said it was because they had been taught to be prejudiced.

When corporate executives of a major U.S. corporation referred to African Americans as niggers or as black jelly beans (Roberts, 1998), it would be naive to assume that incidents such as these are the exceptional occurrences of racial prejudice today. They may actually be commonplace. At least, many African Americans believe so.

Neither economic status nor profession makes a difference. For example, it was reported that in March of 1996, police stopped a prominent, well-known African American woman physician for a traffic matter in her hometown. This woman was told there was a warrant for her arrest and was subsequently humiliated by having to lie on ground then walk barefoot into the police station (New York Amsterdam News, March 16, 1996). *"If they'll harass an attractive, intelligent and famous American like this,"* worries an African-American man, *"where does that leave the ordinary folk like us?"*

Although such blatant racism is usually less visible today, every African American wages a constant, often silent, vigil against the persistent blows of racially-motivated behavior.

THE VALUE-ADDED SYNDROME

Even though race and gender are but two of myriad differences among people, leaders sometimes want to know what extras (unique learning styles or different problem-solving modes, for example) come with hiring culturally-diverse people. Unfortunately, this notion suggests these individuals not only must bring whatever skills and talents white men bring, but also something additional.

In reality, differences found in women and minority men can be found in white men as well. The premise that women and minority men bring added attributes (value) to a job does not enhance their stature as it is probably intended to do. Instead, the notion comes across as an attempt to overcompensate for their *supposed* inherent deficiencies. It perpetuates the idea that women and minority men must be better than white men to be equal to them.

Organizational members must accept that women and minority men, like their white-male counterparts, will bring their unique identity, skills, abilities, and willingness to work. They should not be expected or required to conjure up extra qualities when white men are not expected to.

WHITE MEN CAN BENEFIT TOO

Working women and minority men obviously stand to benefit

from the creation of non-hostile work environments. But this book's intended audience is also organizational executives and white men at all levels. Thus, a key question is, what's in it for white men. Why would they want to embrace racial and gender diversity?

This question offers a major challenge of this work, for no matter how it is presented, racial and gender diversity means that other groups want to share white men's long-held entitlements. White men may not be particularly interested in embracing diversity if they perceive that it means others win at their expense.

Writing about their issues regarding diversity, Gordon Barnhart (1996) concludes that white men will embark on an exploration of diversity only when they have a clear picture of benefits—benefits, he feels, that far outweigh any drawbacks. According to Barnhart, these include individual growth, maturity and completeness, greater understanding of human relationships, improved interpersonal competence, enriched relationships, and more.

There have been strong supporters among white men. During one diversity workshop, a Southerner who had acknowledged an association with the Ku Klux Klan had a life-transforming experience. Because he now realized that racial prejudice and discrimination were wrong and had to be confronted, he returned to his Southern town to become a facilitator of diversity workshops. Because he knew first-hand his colleagues' prejudicial thinking and behavior, he was in a perfect position to challenge them.

WOMEN AND MINORITY MEN AS PARTNERS FOR CHANGE

White men may be in the best position to influence positive change in organizational cultures. However, this process is not *for white men only*. Because one element of managing differences is shared ownership, women of all races and minority men must also be involved. They must be able to identify prejudice and discrimination and stay prepared to address them as they surface. Such involvement can be empowering. As proactive participants in change, they are no longer helpless victims who have to wait and hope that others will correct the ills of racism and sexism.

Granted, it may be hard to avoid falling into the trap of victimization. To avoid this trap, women and minority men must ward off the continuing signals they receive of their own unworthiness, for to accept these negative messages is to embody *internalized oppression* (Brown & Batts, 1985). In internalized oppression, women and minority men lose sight of their own capabilities. They may even act out the very stereotypical views that beget and perpetuate prejudice. (This book contains helpful insights on how they can effectively deal with problems they face in organizations, including a later chapter that discusses the responsibility women and minority men have to collaborate with white men toward a resolution.)

BEING MOVED TO ACTION

Few people question that extreme acts such as cross burnings or brutality against women are vicious acts of hatred or prejudice. However, it can be very difficult to convince non-victims that the many subtle incidences that occur are prejudicial, discriminatory— or just as real.

Although most people would like to believe otherwise, prejudice is as severe today as in the past. Under the principle of shared responsibility, everyone has a part in eliminating it. However, there is a catch. If they are to be moved to corrective action, people who are not targets of discrimination must truly believe there is a problem. Add to this challenge the popular assumption that the issues have been resolved, and there exists the potential for dismissal, denial, and rationalization: *"Not that again. There are laws against discrimination. Women and minorities are just blaming prejudice and discrimination for their failures. I've heard it all before."*

Many people make such comments, especially if they have previously attended diversity workshops or heard about stereotypes and discrimination. However, what they may not understand is that attending training, or hearing about issues, may not, in and of itself, engender change. As long as people are not convinced that prejudice and discrimination exist, it makes it easy to reject the assertions that they do. Therefore, this book will offer an account of the realities of prejudice and discrimination that people should find irrefutable. The expectation is that the reader is motivated to action.

CONCLUSION

Racial and sexual prejudice and discrimination continue to exist as serious problems in organizations. If organizations are to move progressively into the future, they must end the conditions that limit employee contributions. Of course, people will have to be convinced there is a problem, and they must feel this problem is unacceptable before they are moved to do something about eliminating it.

Finally, the exploration of diversity should not be entered into as one might undertake intellectual learning on a contemporary business topic. The learning process is a continuing, largely experiential, journey. From a purely intellectual standpoint, people will naturally reason that prejudice and discrimination create major problems for organizations. They may not, however, be moved to action based on this knowledge alone.

Real change does not take place at the intellectual level, but rather at a level where one knows intuitively that prejudice and discrimination are wrong and experiences the gut feelings associated with this reality. A book, by stimulating the reader's reflection, introspection, and self-analysis, can provide only a degree of this level of learning. The rest happens after the book is closed.

The ideas presented in this book can benefit all people— women of all races, minority men, *and* those most central to the process of managing diversity—white men. When every individual in the organization views it as beneficial, dealing with human diversity through principle-based management can become a reality.

The ability to thrive and live under adverse circumstances is the surest guaranty of the future"

Charles Waddell Chestnut, The Marrow of Tradition (1901)

THREE

PREJUDICE AND DISCRIMINATION— DO THEY REALLY EXIST?

Treat all people as individuals, not just as members of a group. Do not prejudge, stereotype or discriminate against others.

Many people assume that prejudice and discrimination are not prevalent in their organizations, that perceptions of sexism and racism are the products of overactive imaginations or things of the past. Witness these comments heard frequently in diversity workshops:

> *I don't have any problems with women. My mother and my wife are women, and I also have several women friends. None of them has ever complained to me about sexism. At work, I'm sure not taking any opportunities away from women; I see them climbing ahead with no problem. Women are already free and equal.*

or...

> *Why should I take the blame for something that happened way back in history? I didn't have anything to do with slavery. I should not be blamed today for something my great, great grandfather may have done. I never owned any slaves. I'm not a member of the Ku Klux Klan.*

Rarely does a person acknowledge his or her prejudices. In dozens of workshops or interpersonal conversations, I have seen few people readily admit to being prejudiced. They sincerely do not believe they are. *"I don't have a prejudiced bone in my body. I treat everyone the same,"* they say.

As I arrived at my hotel one morning after a jog dressed in a sweat suit, I feel certain that the young white woman who approached me and asked me to put her bags on the airport bus, did not think she was being prejudiced in mistaking me, an African American woman, for the bus driver. After all, as she probably told herself, this was an innocent mistake. No harm done, really. This woman and I had attended the same seminar at that very hotel.

Usually after going through sensitivity exercises, people will begrudgingly acknowledge having some biases. However, it can be very painful to make such a personal disclosure, and to mitigate the pain, they resort to rationalizing: *"I may have some biases, but they surely don't hurt anybody. Besides, doesn't everybody?"*

People are products of their environments, and American culture has produced a society of prejudiced people. Although legislation prohibits outright segregation and discrimination, eliminating prejudicial attitudes which lead to discrimination cannot be legislated. This will happen only as people examine their belief systems, recognize their biases, and work to change their thinking.

But few people will be interested in seeking resolution to a problem they do not believe is real. Unless prejudicial actions are inarguably blatant, conspicuous, and visible, it is easier, and far more comfortable, to just deny that they exist.

What most people may not realize is that blatant acts of prejudice and discrimination are *the exception.* A significant majority of acts are subtle and invisible, a factor that adds greatly to their ability to do harm since they are often evident only after there has been an occurrence and the damage is already done.

In spite of what many non-targeted people may feel, most women and minority men will say that prejudice and discrimination do exist. Not only that, they experience it regularly. Although a study of prejudice against African Americans in the U.S. from 1972 to 1984 suggested a decline during this period (Cox, 1993), this is not what African Americans reported. In the same study, twice as many African Americans as whites believed that racism had actually *increased.*

Ann Morrison (1992) found thirteen distinct barriers to advancement for women and minority men in organizations. Of these, prejudice was number one.

"I never really experienced any problems as a woman until I moved into the upper levels," said a senior white-woman manager, one of the few at her level in the organization. This woman expressed chagrin at experiencing, for the first time, some of the negative fallout of prejudice and discrimination:

> *The environment is different at the top. My peers are now much more competitive than before, not as collaborative or supportive as I had hoped. I sense they have more of a problem dealing with a woman at this level than I would have expected.*

In organizations today, few women or minority men are lucky enough to escape prejudice and discrimination. Witness the perspective of a group of black and white corporate managers:

> *Our vision for diversity is that there will be a time when we won't have to have discussions about diversity—that it will be a natural part of how we do business... Where the words of Dr. King's 'I Have A Dream' speech are as meaningful to whites as they are to blacks... That this company will be a place where differences, certainly those that are cultural differences—race and sex in particular—won't make a difference.*

Although these speakers were specifically addressing black and white issues, they could just as easily have been talking about any culturally diverse group, as none has gone completely untouched by prejudice.

Prejudice against others can become such a cultural norm that it takes on a life of its own (Tajfel, 1970). It can also be elusive since people can be prejudiced but completely unaware that they are.

YOU CALL THAT DISCRIMINATION?

Many victims of prejudice feel that others do not believe them when they describe discrimination (Blank & Slipp, 1994). One of the most frustrating challenges people face is putting their experiences into words others can understand and accept as real. This challenge is made more difficult since few experiences affect exclusively one group or another. This makes it easy for people to dismiss what they hear.

One black woman told of being passed over during meal service on an airplane as she sat waiting in a window seat with her tray table down ready to receive her meal. Meals were handed to every one around her, including her traveling partner, a white woman who was seated in the aisle seat of the same row.

Puzzled, her business companion asked the black woman if she had notified the airline attendant that she did not wish to be served. She had not. Eventually, she received her meal only after summoning the white flight attendant who, embarrassed, offered a weak apology: *"I'm sorry, I didn't see you."*

"You call that discrimination? Why, the same thing happened to me once on a plane," was the reply of the unconvinced white man. He added:

> *"I think you are being way too sensitive. Come on now. Do you really think someone would do something like that deliberately?"*

Whether or not it was deliberate was not the point. Explained the woman, *"The fact that this attendant could look right at me and not see anyone—that, to me, is the problem."* The white man remained unconvinced.

When prejudicial behavior occurs in organizations, vital human resources are lost and the organization cannot operate at its fullest capacity.

SUBTLE BIASES: IMPACT ON THE CORPORATE CLIMATE

Many people have attended diversity training where the primary objective is to help people understand how beliefs and attitudes affect behavior. However, all too often, valuable time is spent trying to convince people that prejudice and discrimination exist and not just in other people.

A particular workshop exercise has been very effective in this regard. Participants are asked to answer questions about four individuals for whom a very limited profile is provided. For each question, they have the choice of two answers—one objective, and the other laced with a hidden stereotype.

Participants do not know there are two sets of profiles. Half of the participants receive additional information—either the person's race, age, gender, or ethnicity. The answers, not surprisingly, are always as different as night and day. In every case, answers based on additional data are *skewed toward prevalent stereotypical beliefs.*

A brief summary of one of the profiles will explain further. One profile simply described a person as a *twenty-eight-year-old male who resided in Chicago.* Questions centered on his preference in cars (Toyota or Cadillac), employment (automobile mechanic or accountant), religious background (Baptist or Episcopal), clothing (dark and conservative or flashy and bright), and sports (basketball or tennis).

The answers from the participants who did not have an additional demographic data point possibly reflected their personal preferences and values. Thus, they typically answered that this man drove a Toyota, was an accountant, an Episcopalian, and preferred conservative dark colors and tennis.

However, answers from the group who knew the man was black were fraught with stereotypes. This man was now a Cadillac driver, an automobile mechanic, a Baptist who wore flashy, bright colors and preferred basketball.

The people with additional demographic information rated their confidence in their answers as much as twice as high as those who did not have this information. This pattern occurred with each of the other types of difference—gender, age, and ethnicity. The exercise handily convinced participants that, indeed, stereotypes truly exist, even among the people in the room.

So, what is wrong with basketball and being a Baptist? The problem is that people do not check their opinions at the door when they enter the workplace. So into the workplace they come— influencing decision-making and interpersonal interactions.

It would be naive to assume that people with stereotypical beliefs about African Americans, women of all other races, other ethnic groups, or older people, do not exercise these beliefs in the daily conduct of business. How might this show up at work? For one thing, if people have a mental profile of the successful employee, those who do not fit this profile, for whatever reason, may not be considered as effective as those who do. It is unlikely that a staffing choice for an accountant's position would be a black male prejudged by the interviewer to be the automobile-mechanic type. (Besides, he just might arrive at work dressed in flashy, bright colors.)

While this example may seem farfetched, it still indicates how stereotypical opinions and beliefs can be acted upon in the workplace.

When dealing with their subordinates, most managers think they make fair, unbiased, informed decisions and evaluations. In reality, far too many organizational decisions regarding staffing, performance and discipline are made only after the race and gender of the person being considered are known.

A study in which leaders were asked to make routine management decisions cites evidence of powerful but subtle biases in the workplace (Rosen & Jerdee, 1974). Fifteen hundred subscribers to *The Harvard Business Review* were surveyed. Fewer than six percent were women.

These managers were asked to respond to a questionnaire designed to sample executive decision-making pertaining to such things as promotion, development, travel opportunities, and disciplinary procedures.

Two versions of the questionnaire which featured men and women in approximately an equal number of cases, were issued. Respondents had no way of knowing that others were evaluating the identical scenarios, but with one fundamental difference—the gender of the employees.

The scenarios were situations that might ordinarily be encountered in an average organization. One involved an employee with a tardiness problem. Respondents were given different strategies for handling this employee, strategies that ranged from disciplining the individual to not making an issue of it.

The results showed that the majority was in favor of suspending or threatening to fire the female employee, whereas respondents whose problem employee was a male were more tolerant. Responses from all scenarios favored male employees. Overall, the survey concluded there was *greater organizational concern and support for male employees than female employees.*

This survey took place in 1974. However, in the early 1990's, a similar survey used in a diversity-awareness exercise at a major corporation reflected the 1974 findings: decisions generally favored male employees over female employees.

As an example, one scenario involved deciding which person was to be given a training opportunity—a bright new manager with developmental potential or a senior manager not on track for promotion.

Interestingly, participants made a case to support the male—whether he was the bright new upstart or the older senior manager: *"I think Andy should go because he is bright and talented,"* or *"I think Andy should go because we need to reward his long service,"* No matter how she was presented, they generally decided against the female.

The disproportionate number of male managers in the work force suggests that the kinds of biased decisions found in these surveys continue to this day.

Workplace Discrimination Happens

At one workshop, a white manager described her experience as the first woman in a predominantly male department:

> I was training for a management role in the plant, a role no woman had held before. When I asked a male colleague what one of the mechanics was working on, he responded sarcastically, "You're supposed to be the manager, you tell me."
>
> He then proceeded to make mockery of my questions, telling other people on the floor, "You won't believe the dumb questions she just asked me."
>
> Obviously, this really stung. As you can imagine, it was not easy for me to ask any more questions. Frankly, I was afraid of looking dumb. My male co-workers never seemed to have any trouble getting the answers and support they needed from others in the department. I had zero support and felt I couldn't win.

This woman later left her job. Although the behavior she spoke of was obviously deliberate, valuable talent is lost when organizational members engage in practices, wittingly or unwittingly, that limit the contributions of their employees.

Another white female shared a humiliating experience when she, her husband, and a male business colleague went to a luncheon meeting at a posh gentlemen's club off limits to women except on rare, special occasions:

> There were two elevators—one on either side of the grand entryway. I was stopped by a man as I was just about to enter the main elevator and asked to use the "women's elevator" on the other side. I thought that was odd, but all three of us took the elevator as directed. My husband and his colleague would

have been permitted to take the regular elevator, but, of course, they stayed with me.

It was only after we got on and it started moving that we looked around and realized we were on the service elevator. We were embarrassed, humiliated, and upset!

Some might respond, *"That's quite a story, but that doesn't sound like sexism. Those were just the rules of the club, and people have to abide by them."* The failure to consider such situations as these as discrimination can be disheartening to women and minority men who often struggle to articulate their experiences in ways others can understand.

Discrimination occurs in many kinds of situations. Take the example of a black person attending a predominantly white meeting. That person may find him or herself being left out, totally ignored or discounted. *"You call that racism? Why the same thing happened to me once,"* may be the response of a white person unconvinced that race was a factor.

Yes, many African Americans would call that racism, especially those for whom receiving a chilly reception at a meeting is not something that happens once, but frequently. Calling this something other than racism may help some people momentarily avoid the painful reality that racist behavior exists; however, it does not make the behavior any less racist.

Discussing the imposed isolation he experienced at a large dinner meeting, one black man said:

At these types of functions, I ... force conversations out of stubbornness. I make certain I talk to people on my right and left at meal functions. I do it because I don't like them thinking I don't belong (Conlin, 1989).

Unfortunately, women of all races and minority men spend too much time and effort developing coping strategies. They often have limited avenues for recourse and are left to their own devices to handle prejudice and discrimination directed at them.

Even people considered experts sometimes offer questionable solutions. For example, one woman complained that she felt slighted because everyone at a meeting was introduced except her. She was advised to address the situation cheerfully, not to offend anyone (LaPorte, 1991).

While that may have been sound advice under the circumstances, if the person excluded from introductions had been a man, the advice to handle it *cheerfully* would have seemed out of place. However, given that this happened to a woman, the advice, which happened to come from another woman, sounded strangely apropos.

One might ask why a woman must make sure she does not offend those who have offended her. Not only does the *cheerful* approach not correct the situation long-term, it excuses those responsible for their intended or unintended rudeness.

One of the most visible ways prejudice and discrimination show up in organizations is in the concentration of women and minority men at lower levels. While there may be a number of reasons for their slow progression, these reasons may all be connected to racial and/or gender bias—lack of role models, networks, and mentors, poor performance ratings, and limited work roles—being placed primarily in communications, personnel, training, and management support (Jones, 1986).

Such work roles as these have not been the traditional path up the corporate ladder. Thus, women and minority men in these roles do not gain the requisite experience most high-level jobs require. Staff/support roles are sometimes labeled *soft* and are not valued as highly in organizations as work more directly connected to cost centers and profit-making. Thus, women and minority men remain frozen at lower levels, and workplace imbalance continues.

NETWORKING AND MENTORING

Since a lack of networks and mentors is cited as one of the reasons for the slow corporate ascent of women and minority men, we will look at these two factors. Formal and informal networking practices, sometimes called *old-boy networking* (breakfast meetings, power lunches at the businessmen's club, golf, working out at the health club, or simply a beer after work), build mentoring and advocacy relationships. Women of all races and minority men are not usually invited to these activities.

Some who have participated have admitted feeling out of place. One woman reported that she boldly injected herself into her male colleagues' weekly poker game. The first time, according to her, was not a fun experience. She went a second time because she felt it had to be better than the first. It was not. The woman described the experience: *"Everyone was uncomfortable. The men's conversation was strained, and they found a reason to break up the game early."* All parties involved, including this woman, were probably relieved when she did not go back.

An African-American-male corporate manager described a particular networking situation of a white-male employee:

> *I could never understand it. This guy was a first-level manager who wouldn't ordinarily have access to all of this information, and yet he was always dropping names about who was getting promoted, what big projects were coming up. He knew something about everything. He even knew who was going to be fired.*
>
> *As it turns out, one of his close relatives was a high-level manager. We figured he kept him up to date on everything that was going on. Of course, everyone treated this guy with a great deal of respect, largely because we all knew of his connection with the hierarchy.*

A mentor, a term sometimes used interchangeably with sponsor—usually a high-ranking, influential member of the organization who has experience and knowledge and is committed to providing career support to an individual—is another factor to consider. Ninety-four percent of senior managers and professionals rated mentoring as important or very important in their promotions to senior levels (Cox, 1993.)

Of his fast rise up the corporate ladder, a high-level white man stated:

> *I was fortunate. I had a powerful supporter right from the start. We had similar backgrounds and interests and hit it off at once.*
>
> *Informally, he began to follow my progress, making certain I came in contact with the right people and got the right assignments, always making sure my name was among those considered for the best positions.*
>
> *It wasn't that it was unearned; I worked my butt off delivering results. But I always knew he was in there looking out for me. This man actually retired several years ago, but even now, I still have the sponsorship of one or two key people in my company.*
>
> *I don't know how I could have succeeded without this level of support. I really don't know if anyone can be truly successful without someone higher up looking out for his career. Of course, I myself have also been a mentor to others.*

Research has shown a positive relationship between having a mentor and career progress, organizational influence, and advancement (Ragins, 1989). It makes sense that having the sponsorship of someone who has already attained success would be helpful. It has been found, however, that women of all races and minority men do not generally have mentors, certainly to the extent their white-male counterparts do.

Some organizations, realizing that these groups face more barriers to success than white men, have established formal mentoring programs. But because of the absence of diversity at the top of most organizations, mentors to women and minority men will most likely be white men.

Research suggests that cross-gender or cross-racial mentoring relationships may be more difficult to initiate than same-gender or same-race relationships (Ragins & Cotton, 1991). Yet, a good relationship is of utmost importance to the success of this arrangement.

Ragins and Cotton (1991) describe perceived barriers to obtaining mentors: women may be reluctant to initiate a relationship with a man for fear others in the organization might misconstrue this as a sexual advance. And men may naturally be more inclined to select other men as their protégés.

Another barrier is that men are traditionally encouraged to take the aggressive role in establishing relationships, while women are encouraged to take a more passive role. This factor may dissuade traditional-minded women from taking the lead in initiating a cross-gender relationship. Finally, women have fewer formal and informal opportunities to develop mentoring relationships as they lack access to many of the informal settings potential male mentors may frequent.

When mentors are assigned, white men should first assess their comfort level in cross-racial/gender interpersonal relationships. The same goes for women and minority men. In the best case, the pair hits it off and begins a healthy, productive association that is good for all concerned. In the worst case, there may be no interest or chemistry between the two, and they may just go through the motions to no good end. Such a mentoring arrangement will likely prove unproductive, not to mention uncomfortable, for one or both parties.

A black woman manager described her experience being mentored by a high-level white man who had been assigned to her:

> *It really was not a very good experience. We met a few times. He was nice enough, but it seemed to me he was usually very uncomfortable. I don't know if it was because I am black, female, or what.*
>
> *After our first round of small talk, he did not have much else to talk about—nor did I. His discomfort made me feel*

self-conscious and uncomfortable, too, and I was glad when our meetings were over.

Sometimes I would call him to 'check in,' but the conversations would be short and sweet. This relationship was really not a good fit for either of us, and I don't think it helped my career in any way.

Of course, I appreciate that he was willing to give it a try, especially since I knew this was probably hard for him, too. But, to be honest, I was pretty relieved when he moved on.

To be a good mentor, an individual must have a genuine willingness to support the development of another. Taking on this responsibility is a large commitment. A prerequisite is that the two people get to know and importantly, respect and feel good about each other. In diversity-driven mentorship programs, if this does not occur, these relationships are working against the odds.

In assigning mentors, organizations should not automatically assume that every white man is capable of developing a mentor/sponsor relationship in a cross-gender and/or cross-racial situation. If an organization assigns white men to mentor women or minority men, it should ensure that these mentors get the preparation they need to be effective.

PERFORMANCE RATINGS

An important factor in placement and promotion decisions is performance ratings and sometimes rankings—comparisons between peers. Since performance ratings are a factor in promotions, a significant gap between the recorded performance ratings for women and minority men and their white-male colleagues will result in women and minority men ending up at lower levels of the organization.

The presumption of women's inferiority to men may make poorer performance the presumed outcome when women compete with men. The same presumption exists when minorities compete with whites. True, lower ratings can be a reflection of actual poor performance since it is certainly possible that some women and minority men, just as some white men, will perform more poorly than others.

On the other hand, top management may not consider stereotypical thinking on the part of managers to be a reason that women and minority men are rated lower than white men. They probably assume their leaders would never make decisions that are not completely data-based. An African-American man suggests this is not always the case:

> *I audited a rating session. Everyone to be rated was discussed individually. The raters were all white men.*
>
> *The proposed rating for a black woman was a "3" (on a four-point scale with "1" being the best rating). There was virtually no discussion; everyone agreed with this rating and proceeded to discuss the next person.*
>
> *Then someone proposed that a particular white man be rated a "3." You might say all hell broke loose. You should have seen these men speaking up in defense of this guy.*
>
> *Several people insisted that he deserved better and came up with all kinds of justifications why he did. This debate didn't stop until this white man's rating was changed to a "2."*
>
> *It seemed to be a question of advocacy. Who was there to advocate for the black woman? Although I was only auditing this session, I pointed that observation out and after some discussion, her rating was also changed to a "2."*

Advocacy in critical career situations may occur much more than most people ever know. While ratings and the ratings process in many companies remain confidential, it is the perception of a significant number of women and minority men that they are, in fact, unjustifiably evaluated as poor performers (Owen, 1993).

At a networking event for African-American women managers, one woman spoke of the performance feedback she had received:

It seems that every black person I know, myself included, has been told, "You're just too low-key. You need to get excited, show some enthusiasm." I feel this means that if I am not making a lot of noise about my work and my results, my boss assumes I am not doing anything.

However, if I started doing this, I would probably hear that I am too intense or excitable. It really doesn't make sense. Other blacks I know have said they received feedback about their attitudes and personalities too. What about results?

Other black women chimed in. Most reported having received similar feedback.

It is difficult to understand how leaders can accept that women and minority men initially recruited as top candidates are transformed into poor performers virtually the minute they enter the organization's doors and begin competing with white men.

On a random basis, of course, it is certainly possible for people to perform poorly. However, when there is a pattern of women or minority men consistently being rated lower than their white male co-workers, the reasons why this is happening should be studied and corrected. Ideally, the evaluation process should be valid, reliable, and less subjective.

As a related issue, individual and group compensation must be checked for disparities in pay across race and gender lines. It generally follows that people rated lower in performance will be at the lower end of the pay scale. Cox and Harquail (1991) investigated the salaries of 503 MBA's of various industries, and found that given equal qualifications with adjustments for other pay factors such as job performance, seniority, and type of industry, women earned less than men.

If a review finds women and minority men earning lower salaries than their white male counterparts for similar work, this must be promptly addressed.

THE DISCIPLINARY PROCESS

A strong sign of prejudice and discrimination in organizations can be seen in the way organizations treat employees who violate workplace policies, particularly if some groups routinely receive harsher discipline than others. This is an important area since many cases charging employers with disparity in disciplinary treatment have been filed in the courts.

Numerous allegations suggest that disciplinary decisions are often based on race or gender. These decisions may be totally legitimate, yet it is also quite possible that some cannot be substantiated.

One way to quickly evaluate the validity of discrimination claims is to determine if a particular discipline is being levied against an employee of one race or gender, but not against a person of a different race or gender who has committed the same act.

A woman cited a clear case:

> *Management was ready to write up a black employee for leaving work early. When it was learned that a white employee had also left early, the decision to discipline was changed. Instead, it was decided that nothing would be done to either.*

One manager described a time when a minority man was to be given a disciplinary layoff for violating company policy. On its face, the action seemed warranted. However, the decision was reversed when it was learned that a white person who had committed the same type of offense had been given only a verbal reprimand.

It has been shown that there is a propensity to discipline black employees more severely than white employees. Similarly, women tend to receive more severe disciplinary treatment than men. Managers may believe they are handling situations on a case-by-case basis and looking at the merits of each. It may be that only after the data are compiled and reviewed does a pattern of discrimination become apparent. Thus, organizations seeking to understand the impact of prejudice and discrimination should examine their disciplinary and other employment practices to see if disparate treatment is occurring.

CONCLUSION

Women and minority men may rightfully believe their next discriminatory encounter is just around the corner. Just as the African-American man described his tactic at a dinner meeting of talking to the whites at his table, victims of discrimination are sometimes given to pretending, or forcing themselves to act cheerful, in spite of feeling the opposite. Meanwhile, the insidious practice of discrimination continues, often with negligible consequences (if any) to individuals who carry out them out.

The potential for improvement in race and gender relations exists when communication flows freely among races and between the sexes. Many women and minority men, however, find it personally difficult to deal with prejudice and discrimination, and altogether unpleasant to talk about these experiences.

They find it especially distasteful trying to convince others that problems exist. Many give up trying. And yet, only when others can see, hear, and agree that prejudice and discrimination exist, will they be compelled to seek a remedy for them.

Organizational leaders desirous of moving their companies forward must create work climates of zero tolerance for prejudice and discrimination. They must design workplaces that do not, by their practices, advantage some groups while disadvantaging others. They must seek out and eliminate all forms of subtle and non-subtle biased behaviors.

Obviously, the subtle things will be hardest to identify, as these are often camouflaged as normal, innocuous events. But be very clear, they are everywhere.

PART II
Discussing the Issues

☆ STEROTYPES: THE ROAD TO PREJUDICE
AND DISCRIMINATION

☆ RACISM: THE BLACK AND WHITE
CHALLENGE

☆ SEXISM: *EVERY WOMAN'S ISSUE*

☆ THE WHITE-MALE DILEMMA

"Intolerance can grow only in the soil of ignorance; from its branches grow all manner of obstacles to human progress."

Walter Francis White (1929)

· Four ·

STEREOTYPES:
THE ROAD TO PREJUDICE
AND DISCRIMINATION

All personnel deserve to be treated with respect and dignity.

n a cartoon, a child asks his mother what a label is. She answers, *"something people put on others so they can hate them without having to know them first."* Stereotypes are labels that shape thoughts, attitudes, and behavior toward others. Gordon Allport (1958) explained that stereotypes allow people to justify or rationalize their conduct toward a particular group. They offer quick, easy solutions to what could otherwise be complex issues. Such generalizing about groups of people, both negative and positive, is a pervasive, worldwide phenomenon (Cox, 1993).

STEREOTYPES ARE LEARNED

Stereotypes have their origins in a variety of day-to-day influences, including family, friends, school, religion, and media. The Federal Glass Ceiling Commission says, *"It is important to remember that stereotypes are not created out of thin air; they often develop, consciously and unconsciously, during our earliest years"* (November, 1995).

Morris Massey (1986) concurs. In his film series *What You Are is Where You Were When,* he points out that beliefs about others are part of early-childhood development and come from a variety of influences, including friends, schools, and families. Edwin Nichols (1991) explains that at an early age, children are outfitted with a pair of lenses that shape their thought processes, values, and beliefs. It is through these lenses that they will view the world for the rest of their lives.

Most people carry into adulthood deeply rooted ideas inculcated during their formative years, but they may have no recollection of why they think as they do. They sometimes react with disbelief when told that family members teach stereotypes and prejudice to children.

Nonetheless, it happens. In a grocery store in a small, predominantly white Kansas town, I may have personally encountered the world's youngest budding bigot. A mother was pushing her infant in a grocery cart. This youngster's entire vocabulary could not have consisted of more than a few words. Yet the child still knew enough words to point to me and exclaim, *"Wook, mommy—there's a neegur."* Obviously, someone had to teach the child this word and its reputed meaning.

Allport (1958, p.272) gives an example of how prejudice is taught at home:

> *Janet, six years of age, was trying hard to integrate her obedience to her mother with her daily social contacts. One day she came running home and asked, "Mother, what is the name of the children I am supposed to hate?"*

A white-female workshop attendee spoke of her early orientation to racial prejudice:

> *I grew up in a very prejudiced home. Both of my parents despised black people and they talked about them all the time. I didn't dare have black friends. My father never had a kind word to say about blacks, or any other group for that matter.*
>
> *I have tried hard not to raise my kids that way, but I know that today I am still the product of my early years. I love and respect my father and it was hard to separate his racial preaching from other parts of him that I loved dearly. I know I still have to wrestle with my own prejudices.*

Stereotypes, once embraced, continue to shape opinions as if they are the absolute truth. A white woman acknowledged that she surprised even herself when she saw how earlier-acquired beliefs affected her present thinking:

> I heard a car coming down the street behind me. The car's speaker was blasting rap music; the loudness of the music was deafening, the beat, overbearing.
>
> I thought to myself, "Why do they have to play that music so loudly?" I pictured the occupants of the car, probably some black street kids with their caps pulled on backwards, no doubt slouched down in their seats.
>
> As the car went by, I glanced over for a quick confirmation and, much to my surprise, I saw two young white teenage boys, their heads bopping to the beat of the music, their caps turned backwards.
>
> This sure did not compute, so I quickly rationalized that these kids must have had some black friends in the back seat and were trying to imitate them. The empty back seat shattered that idea.
>
> Perplexed, I continued to try to rationalize why this was happening; why white teenagers were behaving as I thought only black kids did. They were obviously exceptions.
>
> Only after I stepped away from the situation, did I see how quickly I had stereotyped black teenagers.

Before this incident, this woman said she would have vehemently denied being prejudiced. Some who heard her story chalked up her reaction as an *innocent mistake*, even an understandable one since many people have observed young black teens riding through the streets playing loud rap music.

This woman's reaction may have even been understandable, but it was not innocent. Prejudice plays a significant role in creating conditions that negatively effect others. Unexamined assumptions such as hers play out to the detriment of young African-American males who subsequently suffer higher rates of society's worst problems, e.g., school dropout, unemployment, etc., than the over-all population.

Certainly, prejudice against women of all races abounds. Fueled by negative stereotypes in today's workplaces, men hold most of the power, influence and authority while women are still trying to carve out a niche in the executive suites and below.

Unless something powerful forces us to reshape our beliefs, an experience Massey refers to as a *significant emotional event* (1986), prejudice remains with us.

STEREOTYPES DEFY LOGICAL THINKING

"A riddle drove the point home," a woman said. Her daughter had presented her the following scenario: A man and his young son are involved in an accident and taken by ambulance to the hospital. The doctor comes into the boy's room and exclaims, *"Oh, no, it's my son!"* The riddle asks: So if the boy is the doctor's son, who is the man injured with the boy?

The woman guessed everything from uncle to neighbor, friend, and teacher. Her daughter said, *"Mom, shame on you. I already told you the answer: The man is the boy's father. The doctor is the boy's mother!"* Said the woman, *"I was so surprised to learn that, as aware as I thought I was on these issues, I still just naturally assumed the doctor was a man."*

Brainstorming racial stereotypes during a cultural-diversity workshop, one white male declared, *"Black people love the color red."* Among this racially-mixed group, some white men wore red shirts and one black woman, a red-and-white blouse.

The speaker scanned the room, then pointed to the black woman and with an air of confidence, exclaimed, *"See what I mean!"* When he noticed that several whites were also wearing red, he grinned sheepishly at his nonsensical assertion.

However, making sense has never been a prerequisite for believing in stereotypes. In fact, it is just the opposite. The harmful effects of his thinking could go much deeper, for the man candidly added a real-world possibility: were he in a position to make an employment decision, the notion of someone wearing bright colors might factor negatively in his selection—in certain cases. The negative connotation associated with wearing colorful clothing did not apply, as far as he was concerned, to the white men in their red shirts. *"Well, obviously, that's not the same,"* he said. Prejudice, in other words, defies logic.

Kanter (1977, p. 203) states, *"Stereotypes persist even in the face of evidence negating them."* Stereotypes can be so nonsensical as to interfere with even the simplest rational judgments. *"Holding to a prejudgment when we know better is one of the strangest features of prejudice,"* explains Gordon Allport (1958, p.186).

Allport cites a case from the late 1950's in which a reading test was administered to a group of eleven-year olds. The test was a short paragraph describing a young man named Aladdin, who was the son of a poor tailor and who lived in Peking. Aladdin was described as a lazy boy who loved to play more than work.

The test then asked what kind of boy Aladdin was. The possible answers were Indian, Negro, Chinese, French, and Dutch. The majority of the children answered Negro. Since the paragraph offered clues to the correct answer, it was obvious the children's responses were not drawn from reason.

Instead, the majority of the respondents, even at their young age, apparently based their answers on a prevalent stereotype—that black people were lazy. Once they saw the word *lazy*, the association was made. All reasoning was blocked out.

It can probably be assumed that these children were representative of others their age across the country. It stands to reason that unless their belief systems were somehow significantly altered, these and other negative stereotypes about black people (and other groups) have remained with them into adulthood.

The following conversation between a woman in his audience and Phil Donahue (Multi-Media Productions, Sept. 11, 1981), gives another example of the irrationality of prejudice:

Woman:	*I would not want to live next door to coloreds... I had a bad experience with a black person. I used to feel different toward you people, but when I had my bad experience... my opinion changed so bad.*
Donahue:	*If you had a bad experience with an Irish person, would you be angry with me?*
Woman:	*Yes, I think I would. I really think so.*
Donahue:	*Well, would you let an Irish person live next door to you?*
Woman:	*Yeah.*
Donahue:	*Why? You had a bad experience.*
Woman:	*Because it's not black*
Donahue:	*So black is different.*
Woman:	*To me. I'm sorry, yeah, it is...*

Just as with the example of the red shirts, the rationale to justify prejudice toward blacks did not apply to other racial groups.

Compound such absurdities over lifetimes and generations, and it becomes increasingly understandable that stereotypes have power to adversely impact entire groups. Conversely, positive stereotypes can have the effect of advantaging certain groups. Business and other leaders who understand how stereotypes perpetrate prejudice and discrimination must disallow this devastating cycle to continue.

THE AMAZING POWER OF STEREOTYPES

Practically no group in the world, whether it is women of all races, Hispanics, Italians, Jews, Catholics, African Americans, Asians, physically challenged, overweight, short, or bald, has been exempt from cruel, derogatory stereotypes.

The following examples demonstrate how stereotypes know no limitations. In one case, an overweight white woman said:

People think that if you are fat, you are stupid and lazy, that you don't care about yourself; they think you have no self esteem. They act as if you are uneducated and uninformed, even mentally retarded. They seem to think you don't care about anything and that you have no feelings.

People stare at you as you walk by and then laugh, point and make jokes about your being "fat, dumb and happy" behind your back. It's humiliating and down-right horrible.

A young white woman from the South who had attended a prestigious Northeastern college on academic scholarship shared the advice of a counselor:

With your rural background, you really don't fit in here. You have nothing in common with the rest of these young women. I think you'll be much happier around your own kind.

A short man tells us:

There's nothing you can really do as a short person in a world that reveres tall people. People who are tall are definitely considered superior to short people.

There are all kinds of "short people" jokes like people telling you to stand up when you're already standing. Short men who are strong and aggressive are said to have a "Napoleon complex." Maybe we do. I believe I work harder trying to prove my worth than tall people have to.

Comedians sometimes indiscriminately and mercilessly target groups:

I did a good deed today. I saw a handicapped person parking in one of our [italics added] parking spaces, and I pulled him out of his car and beat the sh___ out of him.

The variety of ways people cast negative light on other groups is unlimited.

A STEREOTYPES EXERCISE

An exercise used during a diversity workshop aided participants in understanding, first of all, that stereotypes exist and
importantly that they can have a devastating effect. As such, they
have no place in business organizations. The premise was that
when people understand that they may harbor harmful stereotypes,
they will be more open to reshaping their belief systems.

Participants were separated into two racially mixed groups of
men and women. One group generated a list of all stereotypes its
members personally believed or had heard about women. The
other group did the same thing about men.

Separately, the exercise was also conducted about race, with one
group generating a list about blacks, the other, about whites. Since
stereotypes can be considered positive, negative, or neutral, the
groups were asked to evaluate each stereotype on their lists to
determine which category it fell into.

Finally, they were to come up with a list of the top ten stereotypes they believed prevalent in their workplace. When finished,
both groups shared their output with the entire group.

Typically, when groups first begin their brainstorming, they are,
understandably, uncomfortable. Participants find it difficult, especially in mixed groups, to blurt out stereotypes about another
group, or even about their own. This discomfort is often character-
ized by nervous laughter, especially over the ludicrousness of some
of the stereotypes. As the stereotypes are called out and recorded,
the group begins to come to grips with the hard-core reality of this
real-life phenomenon, and the mood very soon becomes sober.

As the groups evaluate their lists, especially if they are shaping
up to be highly negative, emotions sometimes are aroused. Some
say: *"Why are we doing this dumb exercise? It will only stir things up and
make matters worse!"*

However, by bringing these stereotypes out of the closet, people can see how big a problem stereotyping is. The brainstormed

lists provide major revelations about how people think about and treat each other. No matter the makeup of the groups, the lists are always consistent.

The following stereotypes about whites, blacks, males, and females generated during one workshop are presented in their entirety. The lists show not only how commonplace and prevalent stereotypes are, but how convincing, not to mention ridiculous. From these lists, we get a real flavor of the negative (or positive) implications of stereotypes in the workplace.

BLACK/WHITE STEREOTYPES

The list of stereotypes about whites is shown in Figure 1.

FIGURE 1

STEREOTYPES ABOUT WHITES

better politicians	in control	slow
can't jump	ambitious	God-fearing
racist	middle class	judgmental
power-hungry	Protestant	bright
more intelligent	drive small cars	technically oriented
smell when wet	flat butts	stubborn
dominating	stable marriages	arrogant
well-educated	always on time	conservative
unfeeling	bigots	two-faced
team player	eat bland foods	good-looking
dependable	industrious	spendthrifts
pick their noses	no rhythm	save money
sloppy dressers	sexist	take initiative
like water sports	poor lovers	Anglo

continued on page 64

STEREOTYPES ABOUT WHITES (Continued)

can't stand hot weather	defensive	WASP
make better quarterbacks	have small families	rich
make better fathers	sneaky	get all the breaks
more peaceable	ruthless	child molesters
career-oriented	fear blacks	white-collar workers
make better coaches	more law-abiding	take care of property
intelligent	superior	frigid
redneck	slum lords	responsible
don't mind cold weather	can't dance	let you down in a crunch
like winter/outdoor sports	church-going	patronizing
born with silver spoons	politically active	gullible

THE 10 MOST PREVALENT STEREOTYPES ABOUT WHITES IN THE WORKPLACE:

intelligent (+)	well-educated (+)
technically-oriented (+)	dependable (+)
responsible (+)	leaders (+)
ambitious (+)	take initiative (+)
in control (+)	career-oriented (+)

Remember that stereotypes are not known for making sense or being accurate. White people, seeing for the first time some of the stereotypes listed, may find themselves reacting with feelings ranging from humor to anger. Still, they gain insight into how other people see them, and also how others handle being targets of stereotypes.

The list ranges widely from positive to negative. Out of 75 stereotypes, 56 were viewed as positive, and all ten prevalent in the workplace were positive. While none of us would want to claim many of the negative attributes on this list of stereotypes about whites, it does not leave us with the sense of despair and hopelessness we get from the list about blacks presented in Figure 2.

FIGURE 2

STEREOTYPES ABOUT BLACKS

all look alike	lazy	prostitutes
athletic	rhythmic, can dance	street-wise
big cars	flashy dresser	promiscuous
lots of jewelry	gold teeth	Aunt Jemima
late	city dwellers	unwed mothers
large families	no father	unemployed
laid-back	reclusive	have no rights
fried chicken/ watermelon	dumb	clannish
religious fanatics	troublemakers	maids
agitators	hard workers	janitors
love soul food	easy-going	shopping bags
thieves	gambling	pink curlers in hair
good singers (blues/gospel)	blues and jazz musicians	can't stand extreme heat
pimps	bad	wear corn rows, plaits
inferior	have tails	can't handle finances
studs	well-endowed (well-hung)	cocky
welfare	wide eyes	rapists
servants	oppressed	shuffle when they walk
like white women	have low morals	jive, bounce walk
poor	ugly	proud
ghetto or slum dwellers	uneducated	untrustworthy
non-professional	menial workers	irresponsible
cotton pickers	sweat	love to party
booze drinkers	big butts, kinky hair	carry knives and guns
superstitious	basketball players	drug users
bar-b-que	lazy	curse

continued on page 66

Stereotypes About Blacks (Continued)

use the term, MF	low intelligence	illiterate
girls, not women	talk slang	macho males
boys, not men	descended from apes	can't be taken seriously

The 10 most prevalent stereotypes about Blacks in the workplace:

lazy (-)	untrustworthy (-)
drive Cadillacs (-)	irresponsible (-)
welfare (-)	illiterate (-)
laid-back (-)	loose morals (-)
can't handle finances (-)	low intelligence (-)

It is probably impossible to not be struck by these extremely negative and vicious beliefs. Indeed, many attributes deemed the worst of humankind are on that list. Non-blacks should imagine how it would feel to have such a list generated about them.

Sometimes when participants see stereotypes about blacks shaping up to be preponderantly negative, they try to turn the tide and have a more balanced list. For example, of the stereotype *Aunt Jemima,* the fat, grinning cook and servant wearing a red handkerchief around her head, one white man said, *"I think she is positive. You people should be proud to have a picture of one of your own on so many household products."*

Reactions to the lists by participants run the gamut from surprise and disbelief to anger and hurt. Said one young, black-male manager:

> *I don't know what to say? I know that I feel pretty crappy right now—not just about the list, but about the fact that my colleagues came up with these things. Is this how you feel about me?*

Comparing the two lists brings additional insight. Unlike the list of stereotypes about whites, of which the majority were positive and approximately a fourth were negative, 80 of the list of 87 stereotypes about blacks were viewed as negative; only seven were positive or neutral. Furthermore, the ten stereotypes selected as the most prevalent in the workplace were all negative.

Many of the negative attributes on the list for whites seem rather innocuous (e.g. sloppy dressers, ruthless) in comparison to the preponderance of derogatory, dehumanizing stereotypes (e.g., dumb, lazy, thief, etc.) about blacks.

This exercise is an eye-opener. Many participants, viewing the two lists of prevalent workplace stereotypes, see how much they differ and understand, perhaps for the first time, their devastating effects. Participants of all races are dismayed at the prospect that they themselves, or some of their very own co-workers actually hold these beliefs or are victims of them.

The groups who generated these lists are not unique from other corporate Americans. In fact, results from the exercise are about the same with every group: the list for blacks always comes out predominantly negative, the list for whites, predominantly positive and neutral.

Marguerite Ross Barnett (1982) points out the subtle political implications of this. In popular culture, advertising, entertainment, literature, and artifacts of everyday living, blacks are commonly seen as slow, lazy, ignorant, stupid, amoral, criminal, unclean, bestial, and generally subhuman. Thus, white political domination and black subordination can be presented as a natural thing, and whites who benefit from (and perpetuate) discrimination, absolved of guilt.

In the film A Class Divided (Yale University Films, 1985), a third-grade student from a small town in Iowa who had never seen a black person other than in the media summed up what he had learned about black people in these prophetic words: "They don't get to get anything in this world."

This child was profoundly perceptive in representing whites' pervasive stereotyping of blacks, some of whom have succumbed to despair from experiencing perpetual racism, prejudice, and discrimination.

Barnett suggests that the extremely degrading perceptions of black people may encourage blacks to accept their conditions and be cheerful, content and appreciative of *having anything at all*, especially when the ideology expressed by the young child prevails, that *"they don't get to get anything in this world."*

The actualization of this belief is indicated in the following account given by a black-woman workshop participant:

> *My husband and I presented a proposal for an exciting, well-planned business venture to a bank, along with our application for a business loan.*
>
> *The white banker looked over the plan and said, "If this report is correct, this would make you millionaires."*
>
> *We acknowledged with pleasure his recognition of our solid business proposal. But then the banker added, "I'll have nothing to do with that!"*

MALE/FEMALE STEREOTYPES

In 1860, Elizabeth Cady Stanton made the following observation: *"Prejudice against color, of which we hear so much, is no stronger than against sex"* (King, 1988, p.43). Indeed, numerous negative stereotypes manifest through prejudice and discrimination against women of all races.

At one time, women, like black men, were denied the vote and other important accoutrements of full citizenry. After a long, hard struggle, women may now vote, serve on juries, own property, etc., yet gender prejudice and discrimination live on.

Examining the lists of male and female stereotypes substantiates this. They reveal a similar disturbing pattern existing between women and men as between blacks and whites.

Again, the lists that follow are actual products of a workshop.

The women's list consists of 46 stereotypes. Just as with black stereotypes, the ten deemed most prevalent in the workplace were all negative. Figure 3 lists the stereotypes about women. Figure 4 is the list of stereotypes about men.

FIGURE 3

STEREOTYPES ABOUT WOMEN

non-competitive	unpredictable	need pampering
scatterbrained	need protection	moody
soft touch	not career-oriented	illogical
slower	can't take criticism	gullible
dependent	followers	Old Maid at 30
gossips	weaker	sensitive
use sex to get what they want	better parent	manipulative
good homemakers	catty	organized
poor leaders	peacemakers	vain
intuitive	cry a lot	understanding
disorganized	nurturing	can't handle money
emotional	barefoot and pregnant	looking for husband
can't drive	indecisive	intellectually inferior
non-confrontational	non-athletic	non-technical
passive	non-assertive	subordinate
less business sense		

THE 10 MOST PREVALENT STEREOTYPES ABOUT WOMEN IN THE WORKPLACE:

weaker (-)	use sex to get what they want (-)
poor leaders (-)	non-competitive (-)
indecisive (-)	can't take criticism (-)
non-technical (-)	intellectual inferiors (-)
non-confrontational (-)	emotional (-)

FIGURE 4

STEREOTYPES ABOUT MEN

dependable	don't carry purses	independent
political leaders	good drivers	thought leaders
better paid	better hairdressers	team leaders
breadwinners	college-educated	dedicated
responsible	logical	strong
career oriented	aggressive/assertive	money-minded
mechanically inclined	technical	intelligent
better with numbers	powerful	independent
unemotional	adventurous	competitive
competent	interested in world events	always drive
strong sex drive	decision-makers	allowed moral freedom
wear pants	cooperative	belong to men's clubs
protectors of family, society	warriors	

THE 10 MOST PREVALENT STEREOTYPES ABOUT MEN IN THE WORKPLACE:

strong (+)	emotionally stable (+)
breadwinner (+)	technically oriented (+)
competent (+)	assertive (+)
career-oriented (+)	good leaders (+)
intelligent (+)	decisive (+)

Results should not be surprising. The list of 38 male stereotypes contained a majority that were positive. More importantly, the ten most prevalent stereotypes in the workplace were all positive.

This exercise was a particularly emotional experience for one white-woman manager. Making an effort to hold back her tears, she read to the group the top ten stereotypes facing women in the workplace. *"I am really trying to keep calm since I see by this list that women are considered too emotional."* She continued:

> I guess I am naive or maybe I've been too sheltered. I
> thought men and women were on an equal footing. It is very
> painful to know that, just because I am a woman, I am judged
> according to such negative stereotypes.
>
> When I look at how women have struggled just to get
> where we are, I guess I chose to believe the reason some
> women weren't making it was because they were just not good
> enough. But I see now that it wasn't just them. A lot of it was
> because of prejudice and stereotypes. This is really upsetting
> to me.

Stereotypes about women cut across racial, cultural, ethnic, religious, and other human differences. Just as minorities enter organizations facing a number of negative stereotypes before they even set foot in the door, the same is true for women.

In spite of women's educational background, prior work history, and other contributions, some people still see them through lenses developed early in life. Take for instance Linda Winikow (1991), vice-president at Orange and Rockland Utilities, stopped by state police on the New York State Thruway. Although she was a New York state senator at the time, they thought her car—with its Senate license plate—must have been stolen since a woman was driving.

Or what about the experience Patricia Hill Collins describes of a woman manager, an honors graduate, who developed a marketing plan. However, before making her presentation, she had to rehearse it three or four times with her manager so he could be sure she wouldn't forget it? Describing the unpleasant incident, the young woman said, *"I sat at lunch listening to this man talking to me like I was a monkey who could remember, but couldn't think"* (Collins, 1990, p.24).

Because many societal messages signal male superiority, it is easy to grow up with the idea that women are not as competent as men. And men, conflicted for embracing more *traditional* views of womanhood, often have difficulty accepting the modern-day working woman, especially in roles formerly held only by men. In many cases, organizational men have wives and mothers who do not work outside the home, yet they must accept their female colleagues on equal footing in the workplace. (This does not happen easily, thus women are among the groups protected under civil-rights legislation.)

IMPLICATIONS OF STEREOTYPES IN THE WORKPLACE

Results of the stereotyping exercise would probably be of little more than passing interest if there were not critical consequences. Because stereotypes influence how people think about and treat others, they negatively affect relationships, employee morale, and ultimately, workplace productivity.

Perhaps every woman has experienced being invisible in a meeting with men, not feeling listened to, having her views discounted and contributions not valued. Whether real or perceived, this experience significantly distracts from a woman's ability to perform the business at hand. Some have said that this type of experience, especially when repeated over and over, has rendered them completely unproductive, or, at least, diminished their productivity for hours, even days.

For the person unconvinced that stereotypical treatment is important to the successful conduct of business, a review of Table 1 below will probably be more convincing. This table graphically summarizes the top ten lists identified in the stereotypes exercise for each of the following groups—black women, black men, white women, and white men.

TABLE 1

SUMMARY OF STEREOTYPES EXERCISE SHOWING BREAKDOWN
OF THE 10 PREVALENT STEREOTYPES IN THE WORKPLACE BY GROUP

Group	Women	Men	Black	White	Total
Black women	10(-)	—	10(-)	—	20(-)
White women	10(-)	—	—	10(+)	0
Black men	—	10(+)	10(-)	—	0
White men	—	10(+)	—	10(+)	20(+)

The above table shows the striking disparity in what different groups face in today's work force. Overall, the picture does not look good.

This table, limited to the ten stereotypes deemed most prevalent in the workplace for each group, does not paint the total picture of the insidious impact of stereotyping. However, by focusing on only ten, the table shows that stereotypes range widely—from twenty negative stereotypes for black women, to zero for both white women and black men, to twenty positive stereotypes for white men.

Obviously, hardest hit are black women who are victims of ten negative female stereotypes and ten negative black stereotypes, thus differing negatively by forty from white men!

This makes black women's experience distinct from the experience of white women and black men, both of whom share an equal number of positive and negative stereotypes. Black women essentially face prejudice and discrimination on two fronts—racial and gender. The effect in the workplace is that upward movement for black women is low to non-existent. (This runs counter to the popular myth that black women, sometimes called "two-fers," are particularly advantaged since they are counted twice on affirmative-action reports. See next chapter.)

Note that white women and black men both have the benefit of positive stereotypes for being either white or male. But zeroing out, they still suffer from prejudices keeping them at lower organizational levels than white men with twenty positive stereotypes. (It should not be concluded, though, that the experiences of white women and black men are identical. For certainly, there is a greater proportion of white women in executive positions than black men.)

As Table 1 shows, graced with twenty positive attributes, white men are automatically assumed to possess an abundance of desirable characteristics when they enter an organization. While it is true that not all white men succeed in climbing the corporate ladder, their lack of mobility is less determined by racial or gender factors.

This exercise indicates huge barriers exist for advancement in organizations for women of all races and minority men. While some do manage to reach higher organizational levels, this is not the norm. Some people erroneously believe that women and minority men break through the glass ceiling because affirmative action forces organizations to place less qualified women and minority men in positions that white men are more qualified for.

JOKES AS A CARRIER OF STEREOTYPES

"Mommy, what has four legs and runs down the hall hollering, 'ho-de-do, ho-de-do,'" my then third-grade daughter asked after coming home from her predominantly white school. Not having a clue what she was talking about, I asked the answer. Proud for remembering the punch line, she responded, *"Two black men running down a hall trying to catch the elevator."* I did not get it. She looked surprised that I didn't and explained, *"They were saying 'hold the door.'"*

Here it was. Racial prejudice had entered my home through the innocence and naiveté of my own child. On that day, my daughter and I sat and discussed the ugly issues of prejudice and bigotry. I am not aware that she ever told another ethnic joke. I do know that, on many occasions, she has challenged other people who did.

For a brief period of her young adult life, a black female friend who looks Caucasian made the difficult decision to pass as white. While associating with upwardly mobile friends, what she found most distressing was their seeming obsession with black people.

Their incessant comments, put-downs, and jokes had her constantly on the defensive. She refused to participate in their tirades, but continually felt angry, hurt, and insulted. She wanted to insist that her acquaintances stop their joke telling. But, she feared that to do so would probably *blow her cover* or cause her to be labeled a *nigger lover.* She hastily retreated to the security of her own race, her brief foray into the white world an unpleasant learning experience.

A letter to Abigail Van Buren touched on a similar situation of obsessiveness:

Dear Abby:

My husband and I are 29 years old. We are friendly with a married couple whose company we enjoy, but there is one problem: They are very prejudiced against black people. This hateful attitude seems to come up in every conversation at least once every time we're together.... (The Sun Newspaper, Baltimore, July 3, 1987).

Jokes. Everyone tells them. We hear them all the time. They can be welcome sources of levity. But when used to cast ill upon others, they can be damaging, hurtful and unkind. Many people question what to do when the prejudice of others plays out before their eyes. Obviously, confronting others is an uncomfortable prospect, and people often prefer to function as if they were oblivious to the harmful acts of prejudice, even when they are the targets of this prejudice.

"Jokes don't bother me," said a 60-year-old Polish man. *I've been listening to people tell jokes all my life. If you can't laugh at yourself every now and then, you're taking yourself much too seriously.*

This man was explaining how he did not mind stereotypical jokes about Polacks.

In his workshop audience, however, some did not agree that derogatory jokes should be treated so cavalierly. Ethnic and gender joke telling, they pointed out, is not funny, but cruel. They cited examples, and the Polish participant began to change his tune. He spoke again:

I must admit, I don't particularly like the jokes, but I can't stop someone from saying what they are going to say. I'm just one person. What can I do?

Other participants recounted insensitive jokes they had experienced and their disdain for them. After a while, the man could keep up his brave facade no longer. Few present will ever forget how he broke down and, through tears, painfully acknowledged he did not like Polish jokes, and in fact he *"hated them."* He confessed:

I've been hearing them all my life. And it hurts like hell to always be the butt of jokes that make everyone think Polish people are dumb and stupid. I've always felt I needed to prove that I'm not just some dumb Polack like the jokes have taught them to believe.

As he wept, others, some guilty of inflicting the kind of pain that now brought grief to this man, others remembering their own experiences on the receiving end of merciless jokes, also wept.

Like him, many people say, *"I'm just one person. What can I do?"* To be sure, confronting a joke-teller can be difficult. It is not easy to gather the courage to confront a peer, colleague, manager, subordinate, stranger or friend.

A white man shared how his confrontation with an ethnic joke-teller brought painful repurcussions. He and his wife had gone on a monthly outing with a group of friends. This group of several couples regularly went dancing, then to dinner together.

During dinner, one woman animatedly exclaimed, *"Say, did you hear the story about the black nun who ..."* This man interrupted to ask if she were about to tell an ethnic joke. Somewhat surprised and puzzled by the question, the woman said yes. He politely responded, *"If you don't mind, my wife and I would prefer that you not tell it because we find ethnic jokes offensive "*

Uneasiness filled the air. Suddenly one of the other men in the group jumped up as if ready to fight and said, *"Well, if you don't like it, then you can just get the hell out of here!"*

The man and his wife quickly decided they would do just that. As they prepared to leave, the woman who had started telling the joke spoke up, *"Please don't go. I'm sorry. I didn't mean to offend anyone."* They stayed but things remained strained among the group.

Since jokes come disguised as harmless and innocent—funny, cute little stories intended only to make people laugh—people may not realize their power to perpetuate negative stereotypes. Therefore, for fear of being viewed as having no sense of humor or being too serious, or for fear of conflict and reprisals, few challenge those who tell ethnic jokes. One white workshop participant said:

> *My father is a staunch racist. I hate to take my kids around him. I just don't want them to have to hear his constant name-calling and joke-telling. I don't know what to do because I would never be able to confront my father, but I also don't want to deprive him of seeing his grandchildren.*

And so impressionable children hear grandfather's bigotry, and very possibly grow up to embrace similar views.

It can be difficult to challenge other people, especially when they feel entitled to free speech. Those who challenge may risk severe repercussions. But, although each challenge might seem small and inconsequential, it can make a difference. As difficult as it may be, everyone must play his or her part.

GETTING TO KNOW PEOPLE WHO ARE DIFFERENT

Some people believe the best way to change prejudicial attitudes is to get to know people from other cultures. It would seem that getting to know others could provide an opportunity to gain greater insight, and, to some degree, it does.

However, stereotyping and prejudice are not logical. Women of all races and minority men have worked in organizations for decades and in non-traditional roles for the past 25 to 30 years. In spite of this, stereotypes, prejudice, and discrimination still abound. Rollins (1988, p.7) writes:

> In spite of hundreds of years of living together as families and in other institutions, modern-day men and women of all races are massively ignorant and uninformed about some of the most basic and deeply-seated issues concerning each other.
>
> This ignorance ranges from basic behaviors that are, in a modern organization, functional or dysfunctional in getting the job done..., to an absence of understanding about basic feelings and experiences generated by working together.

Attitudes and beliefs formed early in life are difficult to reform. Mere exposure to people from other cultures is not, in itself, the answer to changing life-long perceptions. Because of the irrational, illogical nature of stereotypes, a prejudiced person's view does not generally change because of exposure. Instead, what happens is that people who do not fit the stereotypes are considered aberrant, not like the rest. Probably every woman and minority man in non-traditional roles has been told, *"You're not like the others. You're different." "You are more white than black." "You are just like one of the guys."*

A white-woman manager counseled a group of young women:

> Do not feel flattered when you are told that you're different from others in your group. Don't let someone tell "you are

special—not like the rest; just like one of the guys." Be insulted; get angry when you hear this. Do not accept it. Because this type of comment not only puts you down, it puts down all other women.

Will people opt to change their attitudes and behaviors? In large measure, that is the hope. According to Griggs (1995), most people will not value diversity until they consider it in their self-interest. If there are no recognizable consequences for staying the same, or if there are no major inducements to change, it will be difficult for change to occur.

One organization was known for tolerating overt prejudicial acts. Employees were extremely open with telling derogatory jokes. Practically every black employee had heard racial jokes and every woman, jokes putting down women.

This happened in an organization that espoused valuing diversity. A new manager came in to lead the organization. Once he learned of the blatant racism and sexism, he issued a clear message that derogatory joke telling would no longer be tolerated. Anyone who ignored this message would experience severe consequences.

The overt, derogatory joke telling ended virtually overnight. Did people stop telling jokes entirely? That is not known. However, women and minority men were no longer subjected to them. Did it end prejudice at that company? Most likely not, especially if nothing else took place that changed attitudes.

However, this is still a powerful example of how one leader took a stand. What he did was to make his organization an unsafe haven for overt prejudice while reducing the hostile environment women and minority men had to work in.

By taking a close look at workplace practices, including recognition and rewards systems, organizational leaders can determine if there is sufficient reason for people to want to change.

CONCLUSION

Stereotypes play a major role in shaping people's thoughts, attitudes, and behaviors. The male/female and black/white stereotypes identified through a workshop exercise revealed just how cruel, yet widespread and commonplace, stereotyping is.

Even when people are not aware they possess them, stereotypes influence organizations and relationships. If organizational leaders examine the implications of stereotypes, they will surely find them detrimental to the organization's effectiveness.

The process of eradicating stereotypes from organizations begins when leaders prohibit the practices that spread them and harm others.

STEREOTYPES GET YOU NOWHERE FAST!

FIVE

RACISM: THE BLACK AND WHITE CHALLENGE

If people have the right information and believe it to be true, they will generally be compelled to act.

T*hey ought to castrate the nigger and hang the no-good son of a bitch!"* These were the words of a white-male manager at a lunch table of a major corporation. The man was engaged in jovial and animated chatter with his colleagues. So engrossed was he in the conversation, he apparently forgot to lower his voice, and black and white people seated at several of the surrounding tables heard his comment.

His target? Controversial black comedian Richard Pryor, who, in a TV skit the evening before had satirized white people's negative labels for blacks, labels such as *tar baby, jungle bunny, jiggerboo,* and *nigger.*

People within earshot could only wonder how Pryor's skit about racial epithets could doom this comedian to such an ill fate, and was this man's emotional outburst reflective of a deep-seated prejudice, not just toward Richard Pryor, but also toward all African Americans?

Whites hearing his outburst were embarrassed. Some lowered their heads, pretending to have heard nothing; no doubt, wishing this man had kept his thoughts to himself. In daily interactions with blacks, this man had probably concealed his true feelings. But after that incident, they may have found it difficult to work productively with him. (It is not known whether anyone reported this hate-filled eruption.)

This manager's words may not represent the views of most whites. However, even if they represent the views of only a fraction, it still points to a problem. Echoing the words of W.E.B. DuBois,

National Public Radio (1994) reports, *"The problem of this century remains the problem of the color line."*

Beginning with several hundred years of enslavement and genocide and continuing through the aggressive practices of modern-day oppression, the history of African Americans is defined by racism. As it has invaded every aspect of human relationships, American workplaces obviously have not been immune.

WHAT'S IN A WORD? SPEAKING OF RACISM

There is an important connection between racism and the English language. A *Saturday Review* editorial entitled "The Environment of Language" states that language shapes our thoughts about race:

> *Language has as much to do with the philosophical and political conditioning of a society as geography or climate. People in Western cultures do not realize the extent to which their racial attitudes have been conditioned since early childhood by the power of words to ennoble or condemn, augment or detract, glorify or demean. Negative language infects the subconscious of most Western people from the time they first learn to speak (quoted in Moore, 1976, p.14).*

Some of the power of race may be tied to the word itself. *Race* is commonly used to define *divisions of mankind* (Webster, 1990, p. 969). Interestingly, using racial distinctions to divide people is a fairly recent practice, having only been used as the *core for the categorization of ideas about human differences* for little more than a hundred years (Allport, 1958, p.106).

Race is also defined as *a contest in pursuit of supremacy* (American Heritage Dictionary, 1985, p.1020). Defining race in this way could subtly feed concepts of superiority and inferiority with whites being perceived as winners and blacks, losers. Use of race to distinguish ethnic, cultural and geographic differences between people can perpetuate an idea of win/lose. Thus, blacks enter the playing field, by definition, behind the starting line.

Why have Americans embraced the concept of color as an identifier of racial differences? Clearly, no human being has skin that is black, white, red or yellow. According to Marguerite Ross Barnett (1982), the use of color as a classifier of people is an American phenomenon.

The word *white* is generally associated with things fair, pure, good, clean, innocent. Barnett explains that European Americans used white, with its positive implications, to distinguish themselves from the dark-skinned Africans they had enslaved.

On the other hand, the word *black* has mainly negative connotations, e.g., dirty, evil, wicked, bad. Black has been used extensively in English to symbolize negative things, e.g. *black*mail, *black* list, *black* magic, *black-hearted, black* cat, *black* sheep. Then, with the prefix *neg* (which shows up in words such as negative or negate) and a variation, *nig* (as in *denigrate* and *nigger*), the name, Negro, which means black, has suffered the same fate.

Hacker (1992) points out that, since the words do not accurately reflect color, to call a person black or white logically does not make sense. He contends that since these words also carry profound cultural connotations, the use of color to identify categories of people was a strategy to perpetuate the racial inferiority of blacks and the racial superiority of whites.

Perhaps this is one reason many black Americans are moving away from the concept of race as their primary identifier in favor of names such as *African American*, which tie them to their African heritage.

THE MEDIA'S ROLE

What is in a word? Words as powerful tools can generate strong feelings, spark deep emotion, sway opinion, guide thinking, create instant pictures, inflame prejudice and perpetrate negative beliefs about others.

Words have the ability to perpetuate prejudice and discrimination, especially when used by powerful institutions like the media.

For example, more than 40 years ago, in an analysis of 100 movies with black actors, Allport in his seminal work, *The Nature of Prejudice* (1958), found that only twelve movies presented blacks favorably.

More recently, News Watch, a national news-media-monitoring project of the Center for Integration and Improvement of Journalism at San Francisco State University, critiques U.S. journalistic practices on the basis of questions such as the following:

- Do stereotypes, bias, bad reporting, and ignorance distort news coverage?

- How might these journalistic flaws skew what readers, listeners, and viewers of news think about their fellow citizens?

- In what way does this have an impact on the day-to-day activities and decisions of public life and public policy?

The Federal Glass Ceiling Commission says, *"the media do not reflect America so much as shape America"* (1995, p. 46). By merely using particular words, news people can *editorialize* their comments, thereby influencing their listeners while supposedly objectively reporting events. It is not uncommon today, for example, for news accounts of criminal activities involving certain groups to contain "loaded" words from which an audience draws stereotypical conclusions about these groups.

Even if the subject is not pictured, a listener can usually predict his or her race just from the words. This is especially so if the news is negative. On the other hand, positive news items involving blacks or other minorities are sometimes reported with such neutrality that the listener would not know non-whites were even involved.

Consider the following. A newscaster reported that two young white girls, nine or ten years old, claimed a black man tried to kidnap them while they played outside one evening. A man was later identified and charged.

Such alarming news would affirm for many whites what they may have already believed about black people. Whether intentional or not, it would confirm the prejudice of a society that readily accepts, and possibly even expects, such wrongdoing from blacks.

When the girls recanted—they had concocted the tale to avoid getting into trouble for staying out too late—the news commentator described the incident as *an innocent prank*. Words like *an innocent prank* could (subliminally or otherwise) be interpreted to mean that negative things happening to blacks are not to be taken seriously.

Yet, the *real news* is that a man was falsely charged with kidnapping (his life possibly forever changed) and race relations across the city impaired. It is frightening to think what might have happened to the man had the girls not admitted to lying.

The *real news* is that, at a very young age, these two girls already knew how to exploit the race issue to manipulate others.

The *real news* is that the girls' accusation is not an isolated incident.

The words *horrible* and *unthinkable* more appropriately describe this event. It is hardly *innocent*. The reality is that the newscaster's choice of words was insensitive and very possibly offensive to many.

THE EXPRESSION "WOMEN AND MINORITIES"

Most people use the expressions *women and minorities* or *women or minorities*. These phrases are found in nearly every article or book written about diversity. You, the reader, probably use the expression in everyday language. I have as well. For one thing, it is short, easy to use, and seems an appropriate way to identify people who are not white males.

But, in reality, this expression is exclusionary and damaging. If you doubt this, ask yourself who are the *women* in the phrase. Does *women* include women of all races? If so, who, then, are the *minorities*? Men only? Which category—women, minority, or both, represents minority women?

There is something misleading about including minority women in one category and excluding them in the other. It is no better to include them in both categories as if they were two separate classes.

"*I just hate to hear the phrase 'women and minorities,*'" said an African-American woman at a workshop:

> When I hear it, I feel so discounted and slighted. And I wonder, aren't people even thinking about what they are saying? And I'm not talking about any particular user, because I've even heard plenty of us (black women) use the expression without thinking ourselves. Do people try to imagine how I, as a black woman, might feel about this expression?
>
> I feel totally excluded because I believe that by "women," people are really talking about white women, and when the word "minorities" is used, they are referring to minority men. And if minority women are included as "minorities," then am I not also a woman?
>
> Sometimes people even say, "women or minorities," suggesting that I can only be one or the other.

Initially, puzzled looks met this woman's comments. White women and some minority women were unsure of how this common expression could be construed as so harmful. After further dialogue when they finally understood how minority women were, in fact, excluded by this expression, they supported her point.

During a business conversation, someone described a group of six people (three white females, one black female and two black males) as *three women and three minorities*. Three women? Were there not three white and one black women—i.e., four women?

If the *three women* referenced the white women, just where did the black woman go? Was she one of the *three minorities*? If so, did she instantly lose her gender? How did the word *woman* come to describe white women only? If the black woman is subsumed by both words, then she is at once a paradox: a raceless woman or a genderless minority.

Black women face a unique problem of ethnic double consciousness. In spite of many people's beliefs that this group is advantaged because it has two chances to advance (one for being black and one for being women), in actual practice, black women are virtually forgotten in the organizational push to promote *women and minorities.*

In general, it can be said that affirmative-action targets are met by focusing on white women and minority men. Reflected in their low numbers in senior-level positions, black women have gotten lost in the shuffle, a phenomenon referred to as the *"theoretical invisibility of black women"* (King 1988, p.43). Occasionally, if a black woman manages to make it the upper ranks, people assume her rise is typical of all black women. Nothing could be further from the truth.

The stereotypes exercise discussed in the previous chapter points out the unique dilemma of black women being black in organizations dominated by whites and women in organizations dominated by men. Compared to white men and women and black men, black women are victimized by a greater number of negative stereotypes. Patricia Hill Collins (1990) argues that black women's experiences with racial *and* gender oppression produce needs and problems different from those of either white women or black men. Black women must struggle for equality *both* as women and as African Americans.

If target groups are not *specifically* focused on, they can be forgotten. If terminology is not addressed and employment and promotion data not looked at for all races by gender, organizations will, no doubt, continue to ignore black and other minority women. That must not be allowed to happen.

RACISM IN MARKETING

Marketing is at the core of the U.S. economic system. Companies able to make their goods or services attractive to a diverse consumer base stand to gain sales, market share and increased profitability. While this would seem intuitively obvious, some marketing strategies have been (and still are) racist and exploitative.

The label on an old, canned-syrup product portrayed a black man called Uncle Remus with the subscript, *"Dis sho am good."* Many other products were even more derogatory, including *Nigger Head Stove Polish* with its motto: *"This black won't rub off;" Darkie Toothpaste;* and *Gold Dust Powder* featuring the supposedly innocent caricatures of African children in grass skirts.

Other everyday products included *Niggerhair Tobacco* featuring a woman with bushy hair and rings through her nose and ears; an alligator snapping at a treed black man on a box of *Temptation Cigars;* the grinning youngster in over-alls on a can of *Sambo Axle Grease;* and *Smoky Jim's Sweet Potatoes,* featuring a grinning black man holding a bag of potatoes.

These products, which always featured black people in roles ranging from buffoon to servant, were produced from the 1880's to the 1950's (Thomas & Kruh, 1994) when companies were capitalizing on popular racist themes of the day (Barnett, 1982).

As the civil-rights movement brought some of these insulting, despicable practices to light, the portrayal of black men and women in television programs and advertisements evolved into more subtle stereotypes—the wide-eyed young black kids carrying loud boom boxes on their shoulders as they be-bopped along; angry, violent black men; overweight clowning black women.

"Where are the ads and TV programs featuring overweight white women?" asks Steve Barnett (1986, p.48). *"Do some ads that feature blacks reinforce black pride or contribute to black stereotyping?"* The answer is usually the latter.

Barnett gives the following example. While blacks and whites at the bar chuckle appreciatively, a white basketball player in a beer commercial talks about the *feets* of a black basketball star. Barnett calls *feets* a white-invented term no more real in black speech than the word *gwine (going)*.

Only in the last few years has the sprinkling of commercials (for example, portrayals of black celebrities) been viewed as possibly more positive than negative. However, before assuming the problem is resolved, look at a billboard on an interstate highway of a major city. The word *COCAINE* appears in large print across the picture of a prominent black athlete known for a much-publicized drug problem. The name of the popular, white-male singer whose song is being advertised is shown in small print.

This promotion was apparently the radio station's way of advertising itself through a popular new song; however, its message was delivered through a powerfully negative stereotype—that drug use and black people naturally go together. It was a poor choice, one that may have had serious implications for community race-relations.

A 1998 ad-agency memo referring to minorities advised, *"advertisers want prospects, not suspects"* and advocated using budgets to reach *"the more important white segment of the population"* (Harper, p. 1).

Are advertisers willing to risk alienating potential black consumers? Perhaps these advertisers think minorities will purchase their goods even as they are being excluded and insulted. Perhaps these advertisers are not aware that Asians, Latinos and blacks make up a *"roughly trillion-dollar market"* (Harper, p. 1).

Civil-rights organizations and conscientious citizens have raised their voices in protest. Companies and their advertising agencies should take heed. To fail to do so is to alienate large numbers of potential consumers; negatively affect bottom-line profitability; and tarnish public good faith and good will.

Presently it appears that corporate management is motivated when the organization's bottom line stands to suffer noticeably. Organizational leaders, if they operate on the principle that all people are to be treated with respect and dignity, must insist on positive portrayals in television and print advertisements for all groups.

RACE AT THE HEART OF DIVERSITY ISSUES

Because of the numbers, African Americans come in contact with whites many times more than whites encounter African Americans. Thus, blacks potentially face large numbers of prejudicial encounters. Prolonged and ongoing exposure to prejudice, coupled with an American history of enslavement and oppression, has affected how many blacks view whites in the workplace, especially when they continue to experience prejudice and discrimination both inside the workplace and out.

"But I don't have a prejudiced bone in my body" many whites proclaim. Still African-American men and women from all walks of life, including professionals, report frequent and regular acts of racial prejudice: being watched in stores as if they were thieves; not being able to get a taxi in certain parts of a city or hail one at night; hearing the click-lock of car doors by white people as they or other blacks pass on foot; being followed or stopped by police.

At one time or another, every group has dealt with negative stereotypes and discrimination. However, few prejudices have persisted to the degree prejudice against African Americans has. *"I must admit, I am not comfortable around blacks,"* said a Japanese man speaking at a cultural-diversity workshop. This man, who had been in the U.S. for many of his adult years, was explaining that other groups, including the Japanese, experience prejudice and discrimination, too.

However, feelings against African Americans seemed common even in these groups. Said this Japanese man:

> Since I have been in this country, I have had some personal experiences being stereotyped. But even though I knew little about black Americans from direct experience, I learned to have a different attitude toward blacks even before I came to America.
>
> In my country, all Westerners were different. But those with dark skin were often looked upon as even greater oddities.

When I came to the United States, it did not take long for me to be accepted by whites, at least to some degree. Even though they are native citizens of this country, I do not see blacks being accepted by whites in the same way as I have been accepted.

Many African Americans are extremely puzzled at being shunned by other non-white races. One African American talked about his Asian brother-in-law who told him that when he was not with his black wife, whites treated him as white and included him in gatherings. However, when he was with his wife, they mostly ignored, or more accurately, stared at him but did not invite him into their circles.

At a management-development workshop where the diversity segment focused entirely on male/female and black/white issues, some participants complained, *"There are other ethnic groups here. Why focus only on blacks?"* Several participants from Mexico expressed similar concerns.

Based on this input, the conveners decided to modify *future* designs. The next day they were surprised at what they heard. The consensus was that the previous day's diversity segment should not be changed after all. A participant from Mexico said:

I have learned so much about racial matters, not only between blacks and whites, but about blacks and whites. It even helps me to now better understand Mexican relations with both black and white Americans.

... I cannot think of anyone who would not benefit from the kind of awareness we just experienced about the race issue in the U.S... This session was very helpful; I would not change a single thing.

At this workshop, teams of diverse individuals work together for a week. One team had no African Americans, but was racially diverse, including a Native American and two Asian men (one Japanese and one Chinese). The other six members were white males and females.

Over the week, this team seemed to function as well as the others. About mid-week, however, they asked to meet with facilitators. They wanted to request that black members be added to their team.

Without blacks, they felt they were missing an opportunity to understand an important cultural issue. The Japanese man stated that, while he faced issues related to being Asian and although his team was learning a great deal about each other, they felt they were still only scratching the surface on the issue that took center stage—the black/white issue. He stated:

> Even though I have had virtually no exposure to black people, I can see how they are treated differently in our workplace. I believe it is a much bigger problem than it appears.

A white female in the group added:

> It is disheartening our company has talked so much about valuing diversity, but it doesn't seem to be getting any better.
>
> I recently saw a black secretary in our organization removed from her job. She was very competent, yet her boss said she was not doing her job so he moved her off.
>
> She was left with no place to go and now she is floating around doing nothing of value. She'll probably have to leave.
>
> I am upset about this, but I don't know what to do. When are we going start showing that we are serious about diversity?

Still, another white female on this team said:

> We are always critical of diversity when the focus is on blacks. We'll say: 'What about the poor Indians; look at what happened to them.'
>
> And while we realize that these are serious issues too, we still believe that the issues of prejudice against blacks in this country are unparalleled.
>
> I sometimes like to think that we are making more out of this than it's worth and that the country is not as racist as we say. However, in my heart, I know better.

I'm from Chicago, and I am still ashamed when I remember how so many white people were so violently opposed to Harold Washington when he ran for mayor of Chicago just a few years ago. There were many, many informal negative campaigns against him. He was called all kinds of names. It was not because he was not qualified; it was because of his race. And I don't think things have changed that much.

In one segment of a 1981 workshop by noted diversity consultant Dr. Charles King (featured on the network television program, "America: Black and White"), a young, African-American woman gave a poignant, emotional description of her life as a black person in America:

You'll never know what it's like to have part of yourself, someone telling you from the start that it's wrong, that its bad.

You'll never know what it's like to see someone you love, someone you want to love not be able to reach his goals.

You'll never know what it's like to see your parents, your children, so frustrated they give up and leave you.

You'll never have a part of your human dignity taken because of your color. And that's what it's like to be black (NBC White Papers, 1981).

THE QUESTION OF AFFIRMATIVE ACTION

In the mid to late 1960's, organizations began hiring black people into positions formerly held only by white men. Over the years, their numbers have grown steadily. However, in the thirty-plus years since then, only limited progress has been made in that other problem aspects of their entry have not been addressed.

As previously discussed, black men have had only a modicum of upward movement in many large corporations and black females even less. Furthermore, there is still a disparity in income levels across demographic groups. According to the Federal Glass Ceiling

Commission, African-American men with professional degrees earn 21 percent less than their white counterparts holding the same degrees in the same job categories.

In 1998, 27.5 percent of black families compared to 16 percent of white families earned under $25,000 a year while 26 percent of black families compared to 50 percent of white families earned over $50,000 (U.S. Bureau of the Census). The same disparity was observed in 1993 (Federal Glass Ceiling Commission) and in 1970 (Gray, W. H., 1996).

In spite of being hired into management positions in the last two to three decades, women and minority men managers have often been placed in dead-end staff positions in limited functional areas. Edward Jones (1986) referred to the areas in which they are channeled as *the relations*—community, public, employee and industrial.

Research has substantiated this trend. Cox (1993) describes a study of seventy-six black executives in predominantly white corporations who, in spite of their educational and work backgrounds, were found in affirmative-action or urban-affairs roles. Of these, a majority had technical backgrounds in fields such as chemistry, accounting, or engineering.

A 1987 review of the nation's largest 1,000 companies located only four black senior executive officers immediately below the chief-executive level. By 1995, The Department of Labor reported that only three percent of senior managers of Fortune 1000 Industrial and Fortune 500 companies were non-white. This three percent included Asians, Hispanics, Native Americans, and African Americans. Only three black people (men) are CEO's of Fortune 500 companies as of January, 2000 (Norment, 2000).

Edward Jones' survey of 107 black MBA-degree holders found that 98 percent believed subtle discrimination pervaded their companies, and over half said that the prejudice they saw in their organizations was overt (Johnson, 1987). Although numerous incidences of discrimination in workplaces go unchallenged or unreported, the number of charges filed with the Equal Employment Opportunity Commission indicates an increasing trend. These numbers grew from 28,000 cases filed in 1971 to 149,231 in 1993.

Today, the question is whether Affirmative Action is still needed. One premise is that it has outlived its usefulness, as problems Affirmative Action was designed to correct have been resolved.

Although we would all like to believe that Affirmative Action is no longer needed, many people realize the problem is far from being resolved. In spite of the political unpopularity of this topic, at the 1996 GOP National Convention, Colin Powell urged listeners to lead the crusade against racism:

> *Open every avenue of educational and economic opportunity to those who are still denied access because of their race, ethnic background or gender....always stand for equal rights and fair opportunity for all. And when discrimination still exists or where the scars of past discrimination contaminate the present, we must not close our eyes to it, declare a level playing field, and hope it will go away by itself. It did not in the past. It will not in the future. (Jet, Sept. 2, 1996, p.14)*

A panel discussed the need for Affirmative Action at the 1996 National Urban League conference. One panelist commented that civil-rights legislation would no longer be needed when, based on opportunity and status, white people would willingly change places with blacks, and men with women.

While laws may still be necessary, they will not be enough to correct the problems. To be lasting, change must be system-wide and principle- rather than legislation-based.

WHEN RACISM TURNS INWARD

Sometimes, black people have patterned themselves after whites in their treatment of other blacks. In a workshop, a young black woman who had the appearance of a Caucasian gave a moving example of this:

For the first couple of weeks on my new job, I was warmly welcomed into the organization. White people sought me out to get to know me and help me get on board. They invited me to lunch, and were generally very friendly.

Black women were also friendly, and black men were especially nice. They greeted me each day with a professional, yet warm and friendly greeting. I thought this was a very hospitable company.

I did not represent myself as white and although the subject never came up, I assumed that everyone knew I was African American. When I realized this was not the case, I quickly let them know.

Everything changed. The whites who had befriended me before now avoided me. They had apparently treated me nicely before because they thought I was white, but when they learned otherwise, that all changed abruptly. This was disappointing, but not a new experience for me in dealing with whites.

Black women became even friendlier. But, the most difficult thing for me was the treatment I received from the black men when they learned my race. They, too, changed overnight. Now, instead of a professional greeting, they called me "baby" or "mama" and immediately started hitting on me. It was sad that black men would treat me one way when they thought I was white, but I did not get the same treatment as a black woman.

As participants listened, silence fell over the group. An African-American man was especially troubled over the way black men had treated this woman. He realized that he, too, could be guilty of responding more favorably to whites than to other blacks. For him and others, this was a profound realization—and a painful wake-up call.

CONCLUSION

The depth and intensity of racial prejudice and discrimination is difficult for people to confront. Certainly, black people are becoming weary. But ignoring the issues, as many would love to do, will not make racism and discrimination go away.

As Archbishop Desmond M. Tutu says:

"Racism has become endemic.. It is becoming respectable... You must oppose the injustices of racism with a passion—not for altruism, but for your own sake" (June 13, 1994).

"It's a poor rule that won't work both ways."

Frederick Douglass
Address, Boston, Massachusetts (June 8, 1849)

· Six ·

SEXISM: EVERY WOMAN'S ISSUE

Every person, by his or her attitudes and behavior,
is either part of the solution or part of the problem.

... huge numbers of women in [our company] continue to experience severe discrimination at work ranging from comments and jokes to a block on promotion...

In many cases, pregnancy has been responded to in a way that makes women feel guilty. Promotions, salary and career-planning have been mismanaged, not recognizing different leadership styles that many women choose to adopt...

We have been isolated. We have hidden our true selves and, in many cases, had to suppress our true feelings and emotions. This is not only bad for us, it also affects our colleagues, our families and our friends. [We] are perpetuating a way of working that is not the best—for either ourselves or for the business.

> —from a letter signed by female
> managers of a leading international
> corporation

Sexism is a pattern of discriminatory behavior toward women stemming from the long-held belief that women are inherently inferior to men. Widespread and harmful, its effects cut deep into the hearts of women and into the pockets of organizations. The statement above was not written in the 1960's, but in 1999.

Although not long ago, women in management were a scarcity, today their numbers are growing. There has been considerable activity over the years in hiring and placing women into formerly male-dominated positions.

But almost as rapidly as they enter, women have exited U.S. organizations, sometimes only a few short years later. This high attrition rate is one of the by-products of sexism.

SEXISM: HOW BAD IS IT?

It is hard to ignore that there has been racism in America; slavery, segregation and other discrimination against blacks and other races makes it evident. However, society seems less willing to accept that sexism is a serious, widespread problem. *"I am very troubled that people do not recognize the magnitude of the problem,"* says one woman executive.

> *I have personally worked with or encountered countless women coping with the aftermath of serious physical and emotional violence perpetrated against them—rape, relationship abuse, sexual harassment, etc.*
>
> *And unlike what some people believe, this violence does not just happen to certain groups. It happens with all groups across incomes and professions.*
>
> *Some people, unfortunately, have not been willing to recognize how serious and common these problems are—or confront them. So when they hear of highly publicized cases such as rapes in the military, or rape or domestic violence committed by professional athletes, they treat them as if they were unusual.*
>
> *It saddens me that the problem is being kept silent. It teaches victims of abuse and violence to keep quiet.*
>
> *When I hear about the percentage of women who admit to having been subjected to sexual harassment and of things like what the young women cadets at the Citadel said they went through, I wonder, where is the hope that we can ever bring an end to sexism.*

Many people erroneously believe that the problem is not prevalent or that it is the whining of a few victims. As this woman suggests, misperception stems partly from the fact that society encourages women to remain silent about their abuses, e.g., about sexism.

As a result, one of the major problems with sexism is that many of its victims are not even aware that they have experienced it. They mistake its manifestations for *just the way things are.*

Sexism was the subject of a nationally televised news program highlighting the differential treatment of women and men in our society (*Cincinnati Enquirer*, Oct. 7, 1993). Participants were young, idealistic pairs of white college women and men, most who seemed eager to disprove notions of sexism; they did not expect to find discrimination against women in today's world. But what they were to learn was that in every situation presented, the treatment accorded the female participants was different, and worse, than the treatment accorded the men.

One example shown was the scheduling of time on a golf course. In this case, the more desirable times were completely unavailable to the woman, but readily offered to the man—who signed up *after* the woman.

In each case, the woman was treated by the book, whereas the man was treated preferentially. Neither may have known this.

Recorded by a hidden camera, this pattern played out in all scenarios—from job hunting to buying a car. When the unsuspecting participants, along with the rest of the television audience, viewed the playback, they were shocked—the women most visibly shaken. They had thought that sexism was a thing of the past.

During the stereotypes exercise discussed earlier, women were often utterly surprised and dismayed at the pervasiveness of stereotyping and sexism. Although she may not be aware, every woman experiences sexism. Her lack of awareness may show how deeply embedded this problem is.

A speaker at a networking forum for corporate women profiled this kind of woman whom she called *the woman unaware.* She is usually young, bright, eager, innocent, trusting, and, even where others before her have failed, determined to succeed on her own merits.

She has heard of prejudice, discrimination, and stereotyping, but does not think she has experienced them. She believes that some women are just too sensitive. After all, in school she competed with men, studied with them, and overall, found her male classmates supportive.

This woman believes that if a person works hard and gets results, he or she can attain success. All too often, she has no idea of the challenges ahead, nor is she equipped to handle them. Thus, through her naiveté, the pattern of failure is likely to continue.

At this event, two brand new women managers who fit this profile said:

> We don't know why people are making such a big deal of all this. We haven't had any problems. Everyone has been so nice and helpful, especially the men. They seem to be very concerned about us and give us all the help we need. We have always had a supportive relationship with men—whether at school or at work. What is there to be upset about?

THE DOUBLE STANDARD

In our society, a double standard shows up in varied ways. Sometimes when women take on traits commonly ascribed as positive in males, they are seen as negative in women. For example, aggressiveness in women is perceived negatively. When women are assertive, this too, takes on negative meaning: they are considered too pushy. If women are non-emotional, generally a positive attribute in men, they are considered too unfeeling or too hard-to-read. If they are tough, they are considered lacking in femininity, if decisive, too rigid in their thinking.

This double standard speaks volumes about the insidious and irrational nature of sexism, which seriously limits the professional development of women.

In 1997, the average American woman earned 76 cents to a man's dollar (Institute for Women's Policy Research, 1997). According to the Department of Labor, the average female college graduate earns the same as the average male high-school graduate. At the managerial level, white women earned 74 cents and African-American women, 58 cents to the man's dollar (Catalyst, 1997). In 1997, only two and a half percent of the top 2,458 earners in Fortune 500 companies were women (Source Catalyst Fact Sheet).

In 1980, The Bureau of Labor Statistics reported that women held about 25 percent of management positions with less than one percent in top management. In 1995, men still held 95 to 97 percent of senior-manager positions of Fortune 500 companies. Of the Fortune 2000 industrial and service companies, only five percent of senior managers were women (Federal Glass Ceiling Commission, 1995).

Futurist Herman Kahn was labeled pessimistic when, in 1980, he predicted that, in spite of women accounting for 25 percent of managers, it would take about *two thousand years* for them to reach 25 percent of the chief executives of Fortune 500 companies. Kahn did believe they could reach 10 percent of CEO's by the year 2000 (Hyman, 1981). Although by 1997, 10.6 percent of Fortune 500 corporate executives were women, at the beginning of 2000, there were only four women CEO's of Fortune 500 companies. Kahn was apparently being overly optimistic.

One of the reasons there are so few women at the top is that they are often confined to staff positions. Only 20 percent are in line positions that traditionally lead to top executive levels, compared to 89.4 percent of corporate officers who are men in line positions (Catalyst, 1998).

A study of forty-five women in managerial careers who held mostly staff positions (Cox, 1993) found many with limited access and visibility to corporate decision-makers and usually limited discretion, little opportunity to supervise others, limited budget responsibility, and little access to strategic business decisions (Federal Glass Ceiling Commission, 1995).

For whatever reasons, the numbers are a clear reflection of women's slow movement into formerly male-only roles. However, what the numbers fail to reflect are the difficult experiences of

countless women who attempt to find success in organizations, but
leave failing to do so.

GENDER DIFFERENCES IN ORGANIZATIONS— A VISION

At a corporate workshop addressing women's work-related
issues, participants generated a vision of the ideal organization. It
was a workplace where women, while contributing their best to the
organization's success, also thrive, grow, and are valued.

Their vision of work force diversity foresaw business results
expanding ten times as a result of the full contributions of all. It
included an atmosphere of:

- win-win problem-solving
- focus on holistic well-being
- diverse teams generating better business results
- welcoming and valuing of everyone's contributions
- valuing of cultural differences and role-modeling of it by
  leaders
- women functioning at all levels across the organization
- relationship-building as part of the work
- women and men free to be the best they can be
- risk-taking being valued and rewarded

ARTICULATING THE ISSUES

As might be expected, discussing sexism can be difficult. In
many circles, the topic is still taboo. Remember the manager cau-
tioning the woman who complained of a sexist incident to be careful about raising such a controversial issue. This concern may not
be unfounded. Many women cite cases of other women no longer
being around to repeat their stories.

In one instance, a young female manager reported that a male employee constantly leered at certain parts of her anatomy and made inappropriate comments. As a result, the long-time employee received his first-ever disciplinary action. A short time later, the woman left the company, reportedly to *pursue other interests*. The specifics are unknown, but it was speculated that after she reported the inappropriate actions, other male employees joined forces to make her life miserable.

In spite of lack of encouragement, women are becoming more vocal about sexism and in the process, enlightening others. In some cases, diversity-awareness workshops have provided a forum for exploration.

Such exploration can be difficult. Sometimes men empathize with women, but are uncomfortable with the emotions that surface. Other men react with anger or out of fear over the prospect of disrupting the status quo.

Years ago, when it was still relatively safe to vocalize his opinions, one middle-manager made the following statement to two female colleagues:

> *Call me a male-chauvinist pig. I don't believe women should be here in the workplace, especially bossing men around. Besides, look at the kind of money they are making these days. Why, some of them make as much as a man, and I just don't think that's right.*
>
> *My wife sure doesn't work. So call me a sexist if you want. Ha-ha. I still think the woman should be at home and not around here getting in the way of men who are trying to take care of business.*

It seems likely that female managers who reported to this man would have had a difficult time. He has now left the company. However, his legacy of stereotypical thinking remains in some men who manage today's work force, but who know to keep such thoughts to themselves—especially in mixed-gender company.

Many men actually believe sexism is not a problem. But when

they hear first-hand accounts from their female colleagues of the harsh realities and painful effects of sexism, they do not turn a deaf ear. Once they have been made believers, their initial disbelief turns into a strong commitment to end sexist practices.

In one workshop, a middle-management white man listened to women give accounts of sexism. Then he made the following emotional statement:

> *I have young daughters and it hurts me to hear the women in this group talk about their experiences with sexism. As much as I would like to believe it doesn't exist, I know that what they are saying must be true.*

> *I really didn't want to believe this kind of stuff happened at work. I don't want my daughters to have to experience this kind of treatment just because they're females.*

> *This makes me wonder where I've been. I want to go home and talk to my wife. My wife works, but she has never mentioned anything like this. Yet, it's possible that she, too, has had to deal with sexism, and it sickens me to think she may not have felt comfortable discussing it with me.*

THE IMPACT OF SOCIALIZATION ON WOMEN'S SUCCESS OR FAILURE

Jean Baker Miller (1976) writes that dominant culture projects onto subordinate culture those aspects of life (biological attributes) considered the most unpleasant to deal with. Jan Grant (1972) explains that while some qualities attributed to women are biological, many develop as a result of women's experiences in the family, the community, and the economic and political structure.

Morris Massey (1986) says that subtle, value-shaping messages take root early in life. For example, he refers to elementary-school books that read, *"Run Dick, run. Look, Jane, look. See Dick run."* What is the message? Boys run; girls look on. Little girls are praised for being sweet, pretty and coy. Little boys are encouraged to play harder. And so today, according to Massey, Dick is still running—he's running the country, and he's running the major corporations. However, today's Jane is dissatisfied with looking on from the sidelines.

In 1970, Edwin Megargee conducted a study that demonstrated the effect of pressure to conform to stereotypes. He identified groups of women and men with patterns of high and low dominance and paired them to see which would dominate conversation.

In most cases, the expected happened. Groups that exhibited high dominance led the others. High-dominance males led low-dominance males. High-dominance females led low-dominance females. High-dominance males led low-dominance females.

However, the outcome was unexpected when Megargee paired high-dominance females with low-dominance males. In this case, the low-dominance males led the group (Hyman, 1981). This finding shows the power of gender roles and stereotypes.

One could argue that this study happened over thirty years ago; that women today are bolder and less likely to defer to men. One corporate woman's experience suggests that times may not have changed as much as we think:

> I represented my company on a special committee for a major community initiative. This committee was comprised of mostly high-powered corporate women and men.
>
> However, the men on the committee rarely attended meetings. At one meeting that was moving along very well, one of the men showed up. When other men were present, this man was typically a very quiet and unassuming person who rarely spoke.
>
> However, in this particular meeting, being the only man present, he apparently decided he needed to take control. He took the floor and began to run things. He had little to offer and was very ineffective. We did not get much accomplished after he took over.

> *But more importantly, the rest of us just let him run, or*
> *should I say, ruin, the meeting. I really don't know what that*
> *says about us women for letting that happen.*

Sexism profoundly molds American workplace culture
(Hostetler, 1994).

Who is The Successful Manager?

In 1972, a national survey of male and female managers identified the following as the most highly valued characteristics of a person: *decisiveness, consistency, objectivity, stability, lack of emotion, and*
ability to be analytical (Grant, 1972).

At a more recent workshop, women managers identified traits
of the ideal woman. These included *nurturing, sensitive, supportive,*
intuitive, nice, caring, thoughtful, considerate, and healer.

This same group, identified traits of the valued leader—*deci-*
sive, technically competent, non-emotional, logical thinking, intelligent,
tough, and aggressive. (Note these traits are not too different from the
list of highly valued personal characteristics identified in 1972.)

What is significant is that the lists for *women* and for *valued lead-*
ers are completely different while the description of a valued leader
is similar to the top-ten stereotypes (discussed in an earlier chapter) about men in organizations.

Is it surprising that organizations do not value attributes generally identified with women? Instead, it is believed women lack the
innate characteristics needed for leadership. The cultural stereotype
that men make better leaders (Kanter, 1977) is consistent with
numerous studies concluding neither men nor women want to
work for a woman.

What are the implications? The assumption has been that for
women to compete successfully with men, they must be re-social-
ized to take on more male attributes—suppressing or eliminating
attitudes and behaviors considered typically female (i.e., not suit-
able for leadership roles). But they have paid a price. One manager
explains:

When it came to being tough and competitive, I was all of the above. Of course, I also dressed for success. I had no time for women's support groups or other diversity matters, and I devoted myself to the job, playing it as hard as any man.

However, deep down, a part of me wanted to be more myself, have more fun, and just loosen up a little. I suppressed those inclinations so as not to be viewed as weak. I felt that when I was considered 'one of the guys,' I'd have it made.

Did it pay off? Yes, I was successful. I was promoted several times, but my work life was very stressful. After a long while, I finally realized it wasn't worth it, and although it was a tough call, I left. After clearing my head, I now work for myself.

At this time in my life, I refuse to be anything but myself. I feel that I am much more powerful now, and certainly I am much happier. Who knows, I may or may not be as 'successful' as I otherwise might have been, but I now realize what is important to me. Being myself is at the top of that list.

SEXISM IN MARKETING AND MASS MEDIA

Just as with racism, marketing and media play a major part in creating and perpetuating gender stereotypes, in subtle and not-so-subtle ways. Although women make up more than half the nation's population, they are not found in representative numbers in the media.

The television commercial airing that ordinary Saturday morning during children's programming was surprising. The words *advanced teachings for your child* touted the toy a little boy played with. The commentator's words, *"Your son will learn all about math and science"* delivered one part of the powerful message: math and science are for boys. The small, seemly disinterested girl in the background added the second important message: girls don't really care about such things.

The very next commercial was also laden with stereotypes. A dapper, young, male executive dressed for work. His beautiful wife lazily raised herself out of bed to admiringly ask, *"Where did you get that tie?"* Once again, a subtle but powerful message: while the man goes off to work, a woman's place is in the home. Remember, these commercials were sandwiched between children's cartoons.

This was not a unique day. On any Saturday morning during children's programming, in commercial after commercial, females are absent, invisible, or portrayed stereotypically. Cartoon features are also heavily geared toward little boys—full of rough-and-tumble action, male super-heroes, fierce combat, and male athletics.

Commercials like these are a regular part of children's programming. Repeated messages on impressionable young minds create expectations—right or wrong, good or bad—about gender roles.

Other forms of mass media and marketing techniques, casting women as airheads or sex objects, also perpetuate sexism. One of Hollywood's highest-paid actresses received top dollars for her role as a striptease dancer in a movie. Catalogs advertise heavy-duty equipment with a bikini-clad model.

Television sitcoms and dramas, as well as feature films, have also traditionally presented women in stereotypical roles—servile, passive, or weak whereas women who are strong, serious, intelligent, and powerful are less often seen.

THE INVISIBLE WOMAN

Similar to the discussion in the previous chapter about racism turning inward, sexism does too. A survey of twenty newspapers across the country found that only 15 percent of front-page stories were about women in general and one percent about women in politics. These numbers are decreasing despite women being in the newsroom in greater numbers than ever before and despite women writing 35 percent of front-page articles (Tamar Schreibman, July, 1996).

Women, like minority men, still struggle in U.S. organizations. One reason may have to do with numbers. While there is power, support and comfort in numbers, the number of women in many organizations has been relatively small compared to men.

People have sometimes referred to women in non-traditional roles as *tokens*. Rosabeth Moss Kanter (1977) first used that word to refer to the scarcity of women in management positions. According to her premise, their smaller numbers make them unusual in the business setting, and this is a factor in their lack of success.

Snyder (1993) says that beliefs held by men who make most senior-level-promotion decisions determine whether women in management succeed or fail. Only marginally different from the perceptions of more than twenty years ago, they assume that women with children are not interested in promotion or developmental assignments that require them to work longer hours. Further, they believe that women lack necessary leadership skills, work competence, and psychological attachment and commitment to the organization.

SEXISM: WHOSE PROBLEM IS IT?

African-American women have always played critical roles in the struggle for racial justice. They have held *"central and powerful leadership roles within the black community and within its liberation politics ... founded schools, operated social-welfare agencies, sustained churches, organized collective work groups and unions, and even established banks and commercial enterprises."* For this reason, African-American women have not experienced sexism in ways that *"brought white women to feminist consciousness"* (King, 1988, p.54).

Thus, some African-American women believe that sexism is a white woman's problem and that black women's problems are strictly race-related. One black woman expressed it this way:

> As a black person, I don't believe that sexism is my problem. I think that white women are the ones who get the

*benefits from affirmative action with respect to sexism and
gender discrimination.*

*We black women have had to struggle just to protect our-
selves from racial prejudice. If we were to get hung up with
sexism too, it would become just one more thing to keep black
women and black men apart, and we have to stay together.
Our real issue is racism.*

Not recognizing sexism does not mean that it does not exist.
Michelle Wallace attributes what she calls black women's lack of
feminist consciousness to, among other things, their "misguided
beliefs or their inability to recognize sexual domination" (King,
1988, p.54). Yet, problems associated with gender differences are
far-reaching and do, indeed, cut across racial lines.

Remember in the stereotypes exercise when women wound up
with ten of ten prevalent negative workplace stereotypes. The pre-
vailing societal belief that traditionally masculine qualities are better than qualities considered feminine also exists among black men
who, like their white-male counterparts, benefit from the notion of
male superiority (Cross, 1992).

Remember, too, that black women experienced both gender
and racial stereotypes. Patricia Hill Collins (1990, p. 22) described
the peculiarity surrounding black-women issues: "All African-
American women share the common experience of being black
women in a society that denigrates women of African descent.
Black women experience both racial and gender prejudice and discrimination. Sexism is a black woman's problem too." Such awareness is a critical first step in addressing the problem.

One black workshop participant did acknowledge sexism as a
problem:

*I have watched over the years as a few black men were
promoted to levels that, as a woman, I, and other black
women, have not been able to attain.*

I'm speaking about people with whom I feel I could easily

match qualifications. In some cases, I think I was more suited and better qualified than they were, but the system has not yet begun to reward black females with promotions.

It seems that minority requirements are being met by focusing on black men, at least in my company. That definitely seems to be one aspect of sexism, not to mention the everyday discounting and second-guessing I experience in my interactions with people on the job in general.

Of course, that could be racism too, but sometimes I experience this from black men as well as white men. It is overwhelming to face the prospect of having to deal with both sexism and racism.

During a question-and-answer session at a corporate gathering for African-American women, the speaker, a high-ranking African-American man in a key position in their company, was asked why some black men had been able to reach high levels in the organization, but not black women.

His candid answer: *"Black men are able to get closer to the people in power—white men—for no other reason than because we are men. Therefore, we are able to build more network relationships with them than black women can."* The women were struck, perhaps as much because of this man's candor, as his response.

Although women of all races share the problem of sexism, race matters run deep, a factor that creates a significant divide between white women and women of other races. Still, there has been increasing dialogue on the complexities surrounding cross-racial relationships among women. Ultimately, white women must join with women of other races to remedy the horrors of sexism.

If women of all races speak with a common voice, the development of strategies to combat it will surely be accelerated. Furthermore, if Rosabeth Moss Kanter's theory on the significance of numbers is applied, the increasing number of women in the workplace will bring about change. For many, if not most women, change will not come any too soon.

CONCLUSION

This chapter could almost have been developed by repeating complete sections of the previous chapter on racism. Clearly, the problems of gender prejudice and discrimination, like those of race, run deep and wide.

As with racial issues, gender diversity remains one of the great challenges to U.S. organizations. The organization that is able to break through the gender barrier will truly be the pathfinder for others.

The corporate women managers who developed their own detailed vision for the status of women in today's organizations describe it this way:

- Corporate leaders will seek women's leadership.

- The work environment will be harassment free.

- Women of all races will comprise 50 percent of all parts of the company.

- The corporate culture will value *humanness*.

- "Isms" will be absent with one exception—"humanism."

- Women will acknowledge their power and make wise, healthy use of it.

- The comfort level among organization personnel will be high.

- People will be happy and productive.

- The organization will compete successfully in the global marketplace.

We have a long way to go.

SEVEN

THE WHITE-MALE DILEMMA

*No one should be advantaged or disadvantaged relative to others
by virtue of his or her membership in a particular group.*

With diversity efforts directed primarily at women and minority men, organizational leaders sometimes fail to consider white men's concerns. Yet, the resolution of white-men's issues is integral to the success of diversity initiatives.

In the years since civil-rights legislation first called for equal-employment opportunity, white men have seen their worlds change before their eyes. Many have not welcomed this change. This is especially so for ones who believe women and minority men are not qualified, or who perceive affirmative-action to be tantamount to reverse discrimination.

In 1985, white men represented 55 percent of the work force. By 2005, they are projected to slip to 52 percent (Bureau of Labor Statistics). Prompted by fears that they are becoming endangered, many white men feel frustrated, resentful, and afraid (Galen and Palmer, 1994).

WHITE-MALE PRIVILEGE

"So what's to fear?" women and minority men may ask. *"White men still have it made. They certainly have privileges we don't have."* Unlike women of all races and minority men, American-born white men enjoy an exclusive charter to live immune from racial and gender prejudice and discrimination. This is *white-male privilege*—preferential status and benefits bestowed on white men.

Interestingly, white men are often unaware they are its benefactors—or even of what it is. When asked, *"How does it feel to be a white male? How do you feel about white privilege?"* one white man responded, *"To be quite honest, I don't have a clue what you are talking about."*

Herein lies the essence of this privileged condition; no woman or minority man would ever be able to say they do not think about race or gender. In fact, some members of these groups may think about race and/or gender every day of their lives. And they have numerous occasions to think about the privileges they lack.

Jody Miller Shearer (1994), a white man, talks about a white man who murdered his pregnant wife and then blamed the crime on African Americans. As a result, not just one African-American man was arrested; hundreds were randomly questioned or harassed on the street. If a black man had claimed a white man killed a black woman, Shearer said he could think of no city in America that would have arrested, questioned, or harassed hundreds of white Americans.

This is white privilege at its most telling. Combine white privilege with male privilege and we have ready access to American institutions (including their educational opportunities and resources). These are institutions staffed by white people and, in general, controlled by white men. This is a system in which the white man:

- rarely interacts with people who are not white or does so an extremely small percentage of time;
- rarely feels self-conscious or out-of-place (white-male culture and white-male standards are the norm);
- is assumed appropriate for employment in nearly any job and can expect the best pick of them (does not worry about doors being closed because of race and/or sex);
- is naturally assumed to be right or good (therefore, is given the benefit of the doubt when he makes a mistake;
- does not worry about being always accountable for his behavior;
- operates by a different standard than what is expected of people of color and women;

- does not have to seek power for it is automatically bestowed;

- does not feel compelled to respect the rights of people of color and/or women.

Obviously, this listing could continue ad infinitum. What is listed is only the tip of the iceberg. Even if it is woefully inadequate in capturing the essence of white-male privilege, it provides a context in which to think about it.

OK, IF THEY'RE QUALIFIED

A white-male university student said:

> *I think I and a lot of other people don't like it when people want to have their cake and eat it too.*
>
> *They want to say, "let us in for the good of society even though we're not really objectively as well-qualified," and then, once they're here, they get upset if anyone questions their qualifications. (NBC White Papers, 1981)*

Dominant-group members routinely assume that a position is awarded to a woman or minority man because of affirmative action. Yet, they do not automatically question the competency of people who are members of dominant groups (Flower, 1992).

Many white men say they have no problem with the promotion or hiring of women or minority men *if they are the best people for the job* (Galen and Palmer, 1994), yet they have a difficult time accepting that a woman or black man might actually be the most qualified (Elsie Cross, 1992). By stating that qualifications are their only concern, white men may be camouflaging their true beliefs that women and minority men are inherently incapable of competing successfully with them.

Galen and Palmer (1994) suggest there is generally a gap between what white men say they believe and what they may actually believe. Even when they say they would not have a problem if women or minority men were the best qualified, as long as biases and stereotypes are factors in their thinking, women and minority men will never be perceived that way.

During a workshop, a white man was convinced that women and minority men in his company were only hired because of civil-rights legislation. He told a black female who, unbeknownst to him, had graduated *cum laude* receiving a technical degree, that she and others were only hired because of affirmative action. The woman to whom he had addressed his comments was angered:

> *You can't be serious. I worked hard to get the grade and I don't believe I have been handed anything that I have not worked hard for. You insult me by suggesting otherwise.*

> *What do white men have to complain about really? Practically everyone sitting at the top of most organizations and, certainly in the boardrooms, are white males.*

> *When one woman or minority man gets promoted, you always seem to think that we're taking over. Why is that?*

The perspective of many women and minority men is that they are rarely viewed as competent and find themselves needing to prove themselves repeatedly. Explains a white-female workshop participant:

> *I feel I have to prove my worth almost every single day. It doesn't matter that I produce the expected results. In fact, I usually try to accomplish more than what is expected.*

> *I have an engineering degree and an MBA and yet only occasionally have I felt viewed as technically competent.*

> *I never thought it would be this way. In school my peers were mostly guys, and it was great. We studied together, hung out together, and they respected me as a person just like I respected them.*

> *But it's a totally different story here at work. I feel my judgment is always doubted, or I am being second-guessed;*

I'm never viewed as quite good enough. It's not my peers nec-
essarily that I get this from. More so it comes from men higher
up in the organization. This seems to be never ending, and it's
very frustrating.

WHERE DIFFERENCES DON'T MAKE A DIFFERENCE

Some white men believe it is impossible to ever really understand women and minority men. This is a common but generally
incorrect belief. Quite possibly there could be greater similarities
between a black woman and white man who share comparable
backgrounds than between two black women or two white men
who have opposite upbringings.

In fact, there may be no greater differences among women,
minority men, and white men than there are between different
groups of white men. This is a key point in understanding how
people perceive others who are different from themselves. A white-
male manager once responded to this idea with a look that seemed
to say, *"I don't get it. How could a black woman and a white man have*
more in common than two white men?" But he said, *"Don't you really*
mean that black women may be different from each other just as white
men are different from each other?"

He missed the point. Why is it hard to conceive that members
of diverse racial, ethnic or gender groups, because of upbringing,
lifestyle, economic status, or education, could have many things in
common with others, including white men? It certainly should not
be difficult, especially if one thinks about the *white-male norm* and
realizes that all white men do not fit this norm. White men come
from a variety of backgrounds too—some privileged and elitist,
some poor, with many levels in between.

Of course, as long as they believe there can be no similarities
between the races and the sexes, it will probably be true for them.
The problem is compounded when they assume that others are not
just different, but inferior or deficient. The Federal Glass Ceiling

Commission (November, 1995) calls this prejudging a person (usually because of culture, gender or color) as less able to do a job the "difference barrier."

A WHITE-MALE VIEWPOINT

White men who think that equal opportunity constitutes favoritism generally do not have an audience to comfortably share their viewpoint. So, in developing a segment for a diversity workshop, a workshop leader interviewed white-male managers to give them a forum to vent their feelings about diversity efforts, including diversity training and the formation of special support groups and mentoring programs.

Interestingly, the typical response was:

> *I think it's good that women and minorities are getting different jobs. It's about time. Having a diversity of opinions and different styles of doing things makes for a better workplace environment. We are all better because we have to learn to understand people who are different from us.*

One white-male respondent after another gave similar answers. At a time of heightened sensitivity to cultural diversity, is it possible that the men all chose to respond with *political correctness* rather than with openness? Could these men have felt that voicing dissent toward diversity issues would be inappropriate, especially in an organization that proclaimed diversity as a competitive advantage?

During the diversity workshop itself, though, where the setting was more conducive to openness and honesty, a different story emerged. White-male participants were encouraged to put their issues on the table along with their honest feelings. One white man responded:

> *All this focus on women and minorities and the projections of Work force 2000 makes me feel like being a white guy is the worst thing a person could be these days.*

Everywhere I turn, I hear it. Women and minorities are getting all the breaks and all the best jobs. And it is really scary. It's getting so a white man doesn't really have a chance.

Where is the white-male coalition? No one is looking at our issues. We need some support too.

This was one of many responses shared at the workshop. Typically, white men had not been very talkative in such sessions because they usually felt targeted as the bad guys responsible for heaping prejudice and discrimination upon women and minority men.

Some white men said they were afraid they might say something dumb, or that anything they said might be taken the wrong way or used against them. Therefore, while women and minority men generally did most of the talking, white men tended to say little. But this time was different, and, although it took a while for them to open up, eventually they started talking.

As they talked, their often-emotional comments came as eye-openers to many of the women and minority men who learned, for the first time, that not all white men felt powerful and in control. Many said they felt uncertain and fearful. Some of their comments follow:

I don't like what's happening. I'm tired of getting beat up in these meetings. I am not responsible for what happened hundreds of years ago.... I didn't own slaves.

I never tried to stop women from voting. My wife is a woman, and I want her to have the same rights and privileges I have.

I want to be judged on my own merits, and not for something that happened hundreds of years ago....

I look around and see women and minorities getting jobs that I used to be able to look forward to getting. I feel I'm as good or better than anybody else around here. But I don't know what I can expect.

It doesn't matter that much to me to hear people say that white men are still at the top of the ladder. A lot of women and minorities have gone higher than I have up that ladder. I haven't been promoted, and I don't even know if I will be...

I'm a white man, but I don't feel I have any power. I don't think about the so-called benefits of being white. I have always just believed that all you have to do is work hard and the doors would be opened.

But anymore, I don't know, it feels pretty scary. I know I'm not supposed to feel this way. I mean, I should probably be more receptive to other people, but this is how I feel.

In an interesting twist, one white man who had proclaimed early in the workshop that he did not think there really was a diversity problem (he felt women and minority men were using race and gender as an excuse for failure) later emotionally retracted his statement:

I believe I now understand the problem, and I feel very bad for rejecting all that I heard before, especially after hearing how the other guys felt, I can relate to everything they said.

For the first time, I can think about what it must be like to feel this way all the time. Women and minorities have to live with their situations day in and day out. Sometimes we (white guys) can get away from the issue. I'm very sorry for not listening before.

This entire dialogue was a new experience for most of the participants, and, indeed, it was a teachable moment. In fact, participants unanimously rated this as the most powerful segment of the workshop. White men were relieved to have a forum to express their feelings about diversity with no fears of repercussion. Women and minority men were receptive to their honesty.

Without this level of openness, people could have continued to assume all was well on the white-male front and focus organizational efforts only on other targeted groups. Instead of feeling that white men should have no complaints, women and minority men learned that many white men were feeling helpless and vulnerable.

It became clear why white men could not support a diversity initiative that they feared would cost them jobs and status. It also became apparent that if progress were to be made with work force diversity, white men's issues would have to be addressed. Their enlistment and enrollment were essential to moving forward. If ignored, the organization would lose an important opportunity.

On another occasion, a high-level, white-male manager known for his advocacy of diversity issues made the following comment:

> *Many of us have seen how diverse employees can bring a richness to our work experiences that enables us to work better as a team. I have seen it time and time again.*
>
> *When women and minorities are involved, our process is completely different from what it would have been had there been only white men. Generally, when white guys come together, we tend to go along with the program more. We don't question each other, we look at our watches, we may not listen to each other particularly well.*
>
> *But when our groups are diverse, we find ourselves discussing things more, questioning, probing, explaining, engaging.*
>
> *When a woman joined one of our teams, everything changed. Suddenly, because she was different, even our own differences became okay. So her presence brought out an entirely different dynamic for our team. We talked, we listened, and we questioned things more, and I think that's good.*

When this same man was asked whether the result was better because of the effect the woman had on the dynamics of the team, he thoughtfully answered:

> *Not necessarily. But our process of getting at it was better. But more importantly, I don't feel the outcome was any worse*

than it would have been had she not been on the team.

Diversity affects team dynamics. In other words, homogeneous groups are more prone to not see their differences and go along with each other than heterogeneous groups.

It is important to know that group dynamics and interpersonal interactions play a significant role in productivity. If the presence of the woman on this team enabled this group to deal with their existing differences and still have success, the minimum conclusion is that dealing with differences is a good thing.

It is quite possible that the more groups deal with their individual differences, the greater will be the results they attain. Less time might even be spent accomplishing it.

AN OPEN LETTER TO WHITE MEN

The following letter was developed as a joint effort with input from women and minority men from various organizations and levels. It conveys thoughts collected in workshops, support networks, focus-group meetings, and personal communications. Intended to be a one-way dialogue with white men, it includes a general message from the combined group; separate messages from black women, black men and white women; and a closing message from the combined group.

For many contributors, the writing was a cathartic opportunity to address organizational leaders, perhaps for the first time, about how they felt about racism and sexism. Some of their words express hurt or anger; some show empathy and concern toward the white-male dilemma. All genuinely sought to build a coalition with white men in order to improve the organization's treatment of race and gender differences. The letter reads:

&   &   &   &   &   &   &   &   &

Dear White Men:

The cover story of a business magazine (Business Week, January 31, 1994) said, "White, Male and Worried." We now think we understand the title, although we must admit when we first saw the headline, we were very angry—angry that suddenly you were being made the victim.

At first we were upset that you would complain when, in our estimation, you have little to complain about. But at this time we can acknowledge your concerns. We see that future work force projections only fuel your fear of vanishing from the workplace scene.

This may be alarming to you, yet we feel you have nothing to fear. The way we see it, you will probably still be very well represented throughout the entire ranks of all organizations, and this includes the upper ranks.

While we would hope the projected demographics would also mean a substantial number of women of all races and minority men would be able to move up to positions such as presidents, CEO's, board members, and other high-level management, if history is any indication, this will not be the case. In fact, we fear that the only way we will see increased numbers of women and minority men moving upward will be when you join with us in making this workplace more balanced. We believe that in the end, this will make our organizations more competitive.

We are not discounting your feelings, as we now recognize that many of you are scared, and in a way, we hope to allay some of your fears. We think that one of the reasons you feel badly right now is because you are now being categorized for the first time as a group—"the white males" group.

We know this does not feel good because as women and minority men, we have experienced this categorization and all the limitations and injustices that go along with it. While a part of us would like to say, "It's time you knew how it felt," we mostly feel that it is time to reduce this cycle of pain—not to spread it.

We have worked very hard for everything we have accom-

plished in our organizations. However, as we try to see things through your eyes, we realize that you feel you have had to do the same, especially since only some of you actually make it to the upper levels of management yourselves.

Many of you who make it to the top probably had mentors to help you along the way. You realize, don't you, that most likely, we have not. Those of you who do not make the climb to the top probably look around and see the occasional woman or minority man being promoted and, because you may still entertain some old stereotypes and beliefs about our inadequacy, you believe that we are not qualified for this opportunity.

You may even feel that these opportunities should have gone first to you, and that you were wronged when we were awarded what we feel were much-deserved positions.

We want you to let go of these limiting thoughts. They are neither true nor helpful. For not only are we well qualified for the few positions we receive, we also do not feel we've been "given" anything merely because of our race or gender. If, in fact, you did award promotions to us on these bases alone, this, indeed, was wrong, and you have done an injustice both to the organization as well as to all of us.

We assure you that you probably only needed to look around and you would have found women and minority men who were completely qualified for the positions.

Can you remember the discomfort you felt if you have ever had occasion to be the only white male among other groups? Try and imagine, if you will, what it has been like being the "only one," or certainly in the minority in predominately white-male organizations.

We experience this every day, and it really doesn't get any easier. Just as you might have experienced, we still feel that same discomfort regularly. We want you to understand that it has been very difficult facing the daily stereotypes and prejudices we've had to contend with while also delivering good results.

Haven't we given you sufficient reasons to value our presence yet? You should know how much we detest having to earn your acceptance and approval over and over. We think you would feel the same way if you had to spend time proving your competency to us. It is sometimes hard to come into a workplace in which we know we may have to deal with prejudice and injustices. How is it that you cannot see this instead of believing that we are getting "special favors?"

The letter continues with a message from black females:

We feel you do not quite know what or who we are. You have told some of us that we were enigmas. As your co-workers, we probably represent the antithesis of what you were socialized to believe that black people, especially women, were supposed to be.

You choose not to recognize or value the fact that we are powerful leaders and strong, competent, and intelligent individuals. Yes, we feel we are as competent and intelligent as some of you, and more so than some of you.

You are probably not accustomed to having women speak to you in this way, as we believe your own white sisters are not given to this level of frankness with you. But we are taught to speak our minds. You applaud this trait in other white men. Why is it that in us, you seem to find it reprehensible?

So much is said about the quota controversy. We need to tell you our feelings about that. We want you to know that you do not need to hold a certain number of slots for us. In reality, we feel that limiting us to a certain number of slots is protection for you.

For most assuredly, if the best person for the job were awarded the job every time, we believe you would not see the current demographic makeup of our work force. Women of all

races and minority men would hold many more high-level
jobs. Be grateful for quotas, for they protect your interests
more than ours.

Frankly, we look to the time when the best person for the
job will be the one who gets the job. That would open up a
number of new doors for us. This may be difficult for you to
understand, especially if you believe the many negative
stereotypes there are about black people.

Sometimes we get the impression that you expect us to be
extra grateful for the few opportunities that come our way.
True, we are grateful for opportunities we receive, as, perhaps, you are. However, we are not grateful when you occasionally "do the right thing." We look to the time when "doing
the right thing" will become the way you operate daily, and
when that time comes, you can believe that we truly will be
grateful.

As black women, we are strong and resilient, and as such,
we have continued to bounce back from the constant discrimination we experience. But believe us, we are becoming weary.
We are tired of trying to prove that we are "worthy," tired of
being discounted and of not being recognized for our contributions. We presume you are not concerned with how we feel
when we see everybody else getting to the top but us.

We are tired of trying to develop a working, even friendly
relationship with you here at work, only to find that when we
encounter you with your spouse at the grocery store, you look
down at the floor as you pass by.

It angers us that you feel that you must not acknowledge
us in public—that you must ignore our working relationship
when you are with your family members. And it saddens us
that you have taught our white sisters to feel this way too.
Perhaps to please you, they comply willingly.

Yes, we have often contemplated leaving your organizations.
Many of us have done so already. But just as quickly as we leave,

other African American women enter your organizations, and they come with eager anticipation, only to have their aspirations shattered within a very short time as they, too, begin to experience the reality of workplace prejudice and discrimination.

For those of us who remain, we will work with you as our colleagues, bosses and subordinates. But you must know that as long as prejudice, discrimination and stereotypes are allowed to continue, there will always be problems in our organizations. We stand ready and committed to move forward. How fast we are able to move will obviously depend a lot on you.

The letter continues with a message from black males:

In some situations, we feel like you are our brothers. When we fight together in war and play together in sports, we have a bond that allows us to complement and support one another. At times like these we depend upon, trust, and it seems, genuinely care about each other.

However, on an everyday basis, we feel there is more of a competitive atmosphere between us than there is a collaborative one, and in this competition, you seem to be driven to always come out on top, no matter what.

We often sense from you a level of discomfort around us, maybe because of our racial differences, or could it be that you fear that we might surpass you in areas you've been taught to believe you were superior to us.

At times you seem to be threatened by our talents, our intelligence, our common sense, and our capabilities. If there really is a superiority issue, there is no need to put us down through joke-telling, stereotype mongering, workplace discrimination, and through the many negative portrayals of black men in the media. If there really is superiority, why not just let it show up naturally.

We have grown up having to fight ourselves out of the bonds of oppression and discrimination. The character, perseverance, and vitality of black men in the U.S. are unparalleled. We survived the middle passage. We survived slavery. We fought in every war this country has ever engaged in. We sat on the back of the bus in dignity. We began and continue the Civil-Rights Movement. Yes, we are tough, but we feel and hurt, and get angry.

Above all, you seem to be afraid of our anger. The stereotypes suggest that angry black men and violence go together. This is not necessarily so, because if it were, we would only know a world of violence, for surely all black men have been angry.

Daily, we lock horns with the powers and principalities that be, fighting for our very survival—spiritual, emotional and physical. Ironically, some of you have said that you fear that we will try to do to you what was done to us. If this is so, perhaps this may be why you can only be comfortable around us when we are smiling, clowning, or pretending that it does not really matter. Let us tell you, it matters.

More and more, we are concerned about the problems facing African Americans in this country, particularly issues affecting black men. The primary difference between the struggles we face in these organizations and those in the outside world lies in the method of delivery.

Many of the problems have the same root cause—racism, prejudice and discrimination. Even though some of us have found success in your organizations, we can not ignore what is happening to the larger population of black males. There must be an end to the devastating practices that continue to perpetuate the undesirable conditions that are wreaking havoc on our masses.

The letter continues with a message from white females:

Obviously, as our brothers, husbands, fathers, friends,

you are very important people in our lives. We have wanted to support and protect you and, in so doing, have allowed you to support and protect us. By allowing this, you have placed us on a "pedestal" on which we sat and watched—watched as you passed us by, rewarding us with admiring glances.

From this position, wanting to do the right thing, we performed all the functions you expected of us—wife, mother, sister, supporter. From this position, we viewed the world as it, too, passed us by, and secretly we yearned to be more a part of it. We have begun to move away from this comfortable, yet limiting place into new horizons.

As we joined the work force, we first found ourselves traveling the same pathways that we traveled at home, assuming roles as your supporters. Now we are finding these roles to be less satisfying, and through our dissatisfaction, we have discovered what is missing for us.

We have sought and attained educational preparedness enabling us to enter the work force at the same level as many of you had the opportunity to do. We have found a new level of satisfaction, and now we no longer want to be just your supporters; we now want to be your colleagues, your peers. Can you accept us in this way?

Through diversity efforts, some of us have taken exciting new roles, enabling us to experience a level of fulfillment and accomplishment we had not reached before. However, this has not been without a high level of frustration and sadness. We are saddened that we have been subjected to a kind of discrimination in the workplace that no one should have to experience.

We have had to work hard to resist being relegated to the status of second class. We no longer feel it is appropriate for only you to be able to climb the ladder of success. We want to move forward just as you do. We have demonstrated over and over that we are capable, and yet, you have generally not acknowledged this, or have acknowledged it in only one or two of us. This is a painful thing. By not permitting us to contribute at our fullest possible potential, you are allowing a precious resource to be lost.

Yes, your employment systems and practices are discriminatory. Proof: Some of us who are married to some of you have compared salaries. Even if we are at a higher level than you in the same company, in many cases we have learned that your salaries are still higher than ours.

You have to know that it is wrong to let this disparate treatment happen. It is a systemic problem, and it happens all across our organizations. We ask that you will study the data, see what patterns emerge, and start correcting those systems that allow one group to be advantaged over others. We don't think any of us should have an unfair advantage over the others. We believe we can work together to make our organizations more wholesome and healthy for all of us.

Finally, we are not asking for special favors, nor do we want to be treated as delicate creatures who must be protected. If we are to be successful, we need you to afford us a level of respect, dignity and support in the workplace. We value your support, and realize that we cannot be successful if you are not working with us. We can't turn back the clock. Let's work this out together.

The letter ends with a joint note from the combined group:

Our brothers, there is much left to do. We still have serious race and gender problems in our organizations. Ask yourselves, who is winning in this situation? We are being played against each other, compelled to do battle for the few opportunities that exist to get to the top. As we see it, no one is really winning.

Let's stop battling and start working together to change the systems to make our workplaces better for all of us. Let us drive out of our organizations those negative attitudes and *practices that cause so much havoc and reduce our organizations' ability to be completely successful.*

We believe that together we can create the kind of cultural renaissance that will bring the desired satisfaction, happiness and peak productivity into all our work lives.

Sincerely,
Women and Minority Men

WHAT'S IN IT FOR WHITE MEN?

Only when white men realize they have something to gain from diversity efforts, will they be willing to undertake change. Absolutely nothing will move them toward an appreciation of race and gender differences if they only see themselves coming out as losers.

Barnhart (1996) writes that human diversity is one of the great issues of this age, and how people deal with their differences says a great deal about the kind of world that will be created and passed on. As a white man studying how other white men move toward embracing human differences, he writes:

It's difficult to accept that I am, to a certain degree, a "recovering" racist and sexist. We grow up in a society that has strong currents of racism and sexism, and they are a part of our socialization as children, and there are many ways that society continues to reinforce that early conditioning (stereotypes in media portrayals being only one example).

I'm not to blame for my socialization as a child, but I am responsible for how I respond as an adult.

To undertake the journey to full diversity, white men need to believe this endeavor will be beneficial to them as well as to their

organizations. So, what do they stand to gain? A future world
without fears, doubts, or anxieties brought on by racial and gender
tension. A world in which it is finally realized that the pie is big
enough for all, and that one need not feel superior to others to be
happy and productive.

CONCLUSION

If progress is to be made in reaching full diversity, white men's
issues will have to be addressed by organizations. Furthermore,
white men will have to believe that there is something in it for
them. They, like all others, need to understand their prejudices,
stereotypical beliefs and attitudes and determine how these affect
their behavior toward, and relationships with, other groups. When
they question the qualifications of women and minority men, or
describe affirmative action as lowering standards, white men are
adhering to stereotypical thinking rather than allowing themselves
to see the positive attributes others bring to the work force.

Through open dialogue, individuals from diverse groups can
gain insight and move forward in building stronger relationships.
Sometimes diversity-training programs provide a forum for critical
dialogue. However, since learning must be ongoing, it is important
that these conversations continue after the workshops. Unfortunately,
this rarely happens.

Rarely, too, do women and minority men have the routine
opportunity to interact openly or candidly with white-male leadership. The intent of the open letter to white males was to provide a
captive audience with whom women and minority men could share
their thoughts and feelings.

Of course, these views are not purported to be representative of
every woman and minority man's thoughts on the subject. But they
articulate a good deal of what is wrong.

The missing piece, however, is the response of white men.
Perhaps this unanswered letter will serve to foster dialogue among
the groups, dialogue central to moving forward.

PART III
Shaking the Diversity Blues

☆ THE ROLE OF WOMEN AND MINORITY
MEN

☆ A PREJUDICE AND DISCRIMINATION-FREE
WORKPLACE

☆ THE ROLE OF SENIOR MANAGERS

"Lift up yourselves... take yourselves out of the mire and hitch your hope to the stars."

Marcus Moziah Garvey
Philosophy and Opinions (1923)

EIGHT

THE ROLE OF WOMEN AND MINORITY MEN

All organization members have a responsibility to help create the cultures in which they wish to work

This chapter takes the position that everyone in the organization must take responsibility for change, and discusses, in particular, the part that women and minority men play in moving organizations forward. It includes an in-depth look at both ineffective and effective ways of responding to prejudice and discrimination.

Women and minority men must not just look to white men to fix things. For one thing, that assumes they know how when in reality, white men, too, have much to learn. The efforts of targeted groups—their unrelenting passion for fairness and equity—is integral to ending discrimination and prejudice. Women and minority men must not wait for others to correct the problems they face. They must be proactive.

And they must be certain not to collude with or contribute to their problems. This is not to blame the victim. Obviously, no woman or minority man would knowingly contribute to the perpetuation of problems that harm themselves and their organizations. But, as long as they are not proactively addressing the problems from an empowered position, women and minority men are likely to continue being victimized.

WHY DO YOU ALL PUT UP WITH THIS CRAP?

"Why do you all put up with this crap?" asked a white-male manager traveling with two black colleagues. The black man and woman had requested new seat assignments so that the three of

them could all sit together. They had specified that they did not want the last row on the plane. The agent had acknowledged their request, smiled, and issued their seats. On boarding, they found themselves, to their dismay, seated in the last row of the plane.

The black man and woman shook their heads, forced a smile, looked at each other resignedly as if to say, here we go again, and took their seats. Their white colleague was livid at what he considered an outright act of prejudice, and he could not understand why his black colleagues would ever put up with it. He was baffled by their calmness.

They explained that underneath their facade, they were, indeed, upset, however, not surprised.

> We have to choose our battles or we would be fighting every day. What are we supposed to do—get off the plane to register a complaint and miss our flight?

> We don't like what happened; in fact we're steamed. But we have learned not to be too surprised at this kind of craziness. You can't be prepared for it, since you never know how or when something like this is going to pop up. You can't get ahead of it, and you definitely can't out-think it because no one is ever going to figure out all the many things people can come up with. Nor would anyone want to spend all their time trying to. So at least, you try to stay emotionally prepared to deal with it.

How might these two individuals respond from an empowered position when they are probably thinking, "I have no power. I am just one person. What can I do? What can any of us do?"

On the surface, these statements might be seem true, but in reality, women and minority men in organizations do have power. They have power of numbers. (A common voice usually has a much greater impact than a single voice.) But numbers are not the only power, especially in the broader context of capabilities, skills, abilities, and talents.

Still, women and minority men might protest: *"But why should I work to correct these conditions? I did not create them?"* The answer is obvious: If not you, then who? Who is being hurt most by these problems? Do women and minority men not have a stake in ending prejudice and discrimination? Shouldn't you be strategically involved in the elimination of these problems?

Women and minority men must understand how they have come to believe they are powerless. Lifetimes of negative messages and treatment may have taught them to think they are weak and inferior. But, they must repel these messages for they are far from the truth. Through reflection and introspection, they can begin reshaping their own self-perception, reality, and personal power. Then they can join with white men to move organizations toward full diversity.

Of course, women and minority men must be aware there is a problem. Surprisingly, not all of them are. As in the following, the unaware may be in for a rude awakening. After a day interacting with black and white women colleagues, an African-American corporate woman wrote the following:

> *I moved into rage mode last evening as I sat and reflected on the day. I sat at my kitchen table and thought—am I still in Alabama in the 60's. What really got to me was to hear whites say that blacks are still considered not as smart, lazy, and only get jobs to increase numbers or to fill a quota.*
>
> *Then I got even more upset because these thoughts came from managers who are responsible for our careers and our salaries...*
>
> *Will we ever overcome? How dare someone tell me that blacks are not as smart? How dare a white manager admit to me that she's conditioned to expect less from blacks?*
>
> *How long? Just how long must we deal with this? The scary part is that our organization is blazing the trail. Heaven help the other companies...*

I thought in 25 years with this company, I'd seen it all and heard it all. Monday's workshop was the biggest reality check for me in a long time. I've agreed by silence in many situations over the years. It is very evident that I can no longer afford to do that. The pain, the frustration, the rage exhibited by young black women revived my energy to do whatever I can to initiate change.

For too long, many women and minority men have looked to organizational leaders to *do the right thing*. But something important has been missing—their right to expect and insist that organizational leaders address problems with conviction. Of course, many women and minority men have not sat idly on the sidelines. They have taken steps to address these issues. However, permanent success requires the involved commitment of the entire organization, and this can be garnered as women and minority men assume an empowered position that stems from knowing who they are and acting on what they know.

WHY ARE WOMEN AND MINORITY MEN STILL TARGETS OF DISCRIMINATION?

Have women and minority men become resigned? If so, to what can this seeming acquiescence be attributed, especially when the consequences of prejudice and discrimination are so clearly undesirable?

To a large extent, women and minority men have grown accustomed to continuous messages of inferiority. Elkins (1959) theorized that complete subjugation—with others the source of food, money, clothing, shelter, power and authority—produced among subjugated people a childlike demeanor.

As a result, they may respond to prejudice and discrimination in ways that suggest resignation. Believing these problems will always be with us—*they won't go away in my lifetime*—they may accept partial solutions as the best to be expected.

THE SELF-FULFILLING PROPHECY

To a great extent, what people think of themselves has a lot to do with what *others* think of them. Robert K. Merton, a Columbia University sociologist, originated the theory of the self-fulfilling prophecy (Allport, 1958), which was brought to light in 1965 when James W. Sweeney, head of Tulane Biomedical Computer Center in New Orleans, decided to transform a poorly educated black man into a computer expert.

For this experiment, he chose hospital janitor George Johnson to teach about computers. With this expectation clearly conveyed, Johnson became, according to Sweeney, *"just about the best trainee who ever ran the center"* (Loftus, 1992, p.35). This case demonstrates the power of others' expectations.

Countless examples of self-fulfilling prophecies occur everyday. Wishes, fears, beliefs, and prejudices (some of which people are unaware) shape expectations, and these can be conveyed directly or indirectly to others.

A minister's wife, a white woman, thought she had no prejudices—or, at least that she had overcome any she had about Native Americans. Thus, she was relatively comfortable when her husband invited the head of an Indian tribe home for dinner.

When the guest arrived dressed in full regalia, the woman's young daughter jumped around and yelped in excitement. As she continued to squeal in delight, the mother yelled in exasperation, *"Go sit down; you're acting just like a dumb squaw!"*

In tears, this woman shared how terrible she felt insulting her visitor. She had not realized she held stereotypes about Native Americans, but there they were presenting themselves, and at the most unthinkable moment.

It is likely the Indian, accustomed to a lifetime of prejudice, took the insult with dignity and went about the evening. Allport (1958) states that even though they may not mentally dismiss incidents such as this, victims usually manage to react well on the outside.

What is the message in this story? It is that one's expectations are likely to be fulfilled. This woman acknowledged harboring secret fears (expectations) that the family would embarrass itself in front of the Indian. And so, her *expectation* was fulfilled. Scientific studies of the self-fulfilling prophecy have shown that expectations, positive or negative, are a major contributor to results.

Snyder (1982) describes how Harvard psychologist, Robert Rosenthal, and his colleague, Lenore Jacobson, conducted one of the more famous of these experiments in 1960. They identified five randomly selected elementary-school students as *gifted* and so informed their teachers. Because the teachers expected these students to have high abilities, the students performed accordingly. Snyder gives other examples.

In another study, two groups of students were given different descriptions of a lecturer. One group was told that he was warm and caring, the other that he was cold. When asked to rate him, the group that expected warmth and caring rated him as more considerate, more informed, more sociable, more popular, better-natured, more humorous, and more human than did the other group.

In workplace settings, experiments have proven equally conclusive. At a vocational training center, five men selected at random were identified and treated as if they had an unusually high aptitude. Subsequently, these five were absent less than others and learned the basics in half the usual time. As expected, they outscored the other trainees (Snyder, 1982).

Similarly, women and minority men tend to live up or down to others' expectations. Negatively influencing an outcome through others' expectations is called the *Golem Effect*.

The film, *A Class Divided* (Yale University Films, 1985), illustrates the Golem Effect. An experiment was conducted with staff members, mostly white men and women, at an Iowa correctional institution. Eye color determined which side of the room they sat on.

Participants on one side had been told that, because their eyes were blue, they were inferior. On this side, a disrespectful, disruptive, uncooperative, defiant, defensive man scowled at the facilitator. A woman was visibly negative, hostile, and withdrawn. Many others were overtly dysfunctional. As they tried not to draw attention to themselves, some seemed resigned, passive, meek, and uncertain. They all appeared hopelessly trapped and powerless—all since they had been labeled inferior because they had blue eyes.

Participants on the other side of the room, told they were superior because their eyes were brown, quickly assumed the supposed characteristics of superiority. They were cooperative, agreeable, and smug. They exhibited confidence and exclusivity relative to the troublesome group. This group even fared better on a simple written exercise.

Before the experiment, all the participants were co-workers anxiously awaiting a diversity-awareness session. Within minutes, they were transformed into two distinct groups, each demonstrating unfeigned reactions to stereotyping.

Says the film's study guide:

> Placed in a powerless position and accused of being there solely because of a physical characteristic over which they had no control, the adults became helpless, confused, resigned, passive, and fatalistic, and lost their natural orientation toward goals and success (Yale University Films, 1985).

Why the sudden change? Described as unintelligent, troublemaking, untrustworthy, and inferior, these people assume the demeanor of inferiority and powerlessness. Even while knowing they are participating in an experiment, they still act according to the expectations of others. Their behavior reflects anger at being classified as inferior, and, ironically, this very behavior then confirms others' expectations.

It should not be difficult to see how the effects of the self-fulfilling prophecy and the Golem Effect are detrimental to women and minority men who typically have not had the same opportunities for upward mobility in U.S. organizations as their white-male counterparts.

Rosabeth Kanter (1977) describes individuals who have ready access to opportunity as tending toward high aspirations and high self-esteem. They value, even overrate their competence, consider work a more central life interest and are more committed than others to an organization's goals.

On the other hand, people with little opportunity tend to limit their aspirations, do not hope for mobility, or value greater responsibility or participation. They tend to have lower self-esteem; place low value on their abilities; and are more likely to stay put rather than protest or seek change openly and directly.

What does the self-fulfilling prophecy have to do with diversity in organizations? Women and minority men may be the unwitting victims of negative expectations and the self-fulfilling prophecy. According to Taylor Cox (1993), prejudice may do its greatest damage through the self-fulfilling prophecy. Managers who base performance expectations on an employee's class, race, national origin, gender, age, or outward appearance, are allowing prejudice to replace objectivity. They are, deliberately or unknowingly, influencing others' behavior through their negative expectations.

If managers do not expect certain groups to excel, these employees are likely to set lower standards for themselves. Often they develop negative attitudes toward themselves, their jobs, employers, and careers (Loftus, 1992). On the other hand, if management assumes all employees want to and are capable of succeeding, they leverage the self-fulfilling prophecy for a full-functioning organization.

The Relevance of Women's and Minority Men's Self-Image

Women and minority men are often assaulted with direct or indirect messages telling them that they are not as good as others. If they hear often enough that they are worthless, incapable of learning, lazy and unproductive, they may ultimately become convinced of their own unfitness. Oppressed people sometimes internalize the opinions of their oppressors (Freire (1972). Eventually manifesting these messages, they then are subjected to an additional, more powerful indignity—internally driven self-condemnation.

Yet, although women and minority men may act out external messages, they do not neccessarily believe they are inferior. For example, when a woman deliberately allows a man to win a game, it is not necessarily because she believes she cannot win, or because she does not have the ability to win. It may be because she is going along with a rule of socialization: that men, not women, are supposed to be dominant and in control. When black people in the South sat at the back of the bus and gave up their seats to whites, they did so, not because they felt that this was their rightful place, but because of Jim Crow laws.

Speaking on *60 Minutes* (December, 1996) on the importance of Afrocentrism in schools, an African-American professor of Black Studies made clear that black people have no lack of self-esteem. Indeed, they love most things about being black. What they lack, he explained, is the cultural esteem that comes from having their history and heritage valued. This lack of cultural esteem may be at the root of many problems they face.

In other words, when it comes to negative messages, women and minority men may act out these messages while not necessarily buying into them—an important distinction. The presumption that they do buy in may be one of the greatest misconceptions of dominant cultures—and one of the most important in understanding reactions to cultural differences.

After a little white boy called my daughter a nigger in her predominantly white third grade class, the school's older white-male principal listened as I told him what had happened, and what I expected him to do about it. When I finished, he gave me a quizzical look, and asked, *"So, what exactly is your problem?"* He may as well have said, *"You are niggers. Why on earth are you upset if someone calls you one?"*

Might this be how white men feel when women and minority men in organizations do not fit stereotypical expectations? Could it possibly explain why many women and minority men in organizations are sometimes coached to show more gratitude and appreciation instead of an attitude of entitlement?

Both women and minority men say they often receive as much coaching about attitude and style as about performance. A white woman manager, for example, was advised to be more humble. A black male manager was informed he was viewed as too conceited. Perhaps the dominant culture sees their self-assurance and confidence as arrogance or *uppityness*—qualities unexpected and clearly unacceptable from individuals believed inferior.

What many people do not understand is that women and minority men do not usually look at their struggles and failures as a measure of inferiority. Instead, they see them as failures of organizations to deal effectively with prejudice. Many women and minority men in formerly white-male-dominated roles believe they have to be twice as good as white men to be considered for positions in the first place. Their success in organizations where prejudice is absent or confronted substantiates this.

During a workshop exercise, six groups of women, each containing six to seven whites and two blacks, answered the question, *"Given what you know or believe about the opportunities and conditions of the other race, would you trade places?"*

In each group, the answers of the black women were consistent and emphatic: *"No, I would not want to be white."* Of course, the white women also responded negatively to the question of trading places. Having seen prejudice and discrimination against blacks, they felt they could not deal with it, nor did they want to. Others reasoned that they valued their relationships with powerful white men. Some said that they honestly felt blacks were not as good as whites (a statement that bowled some of the black women over).

"I am shocked," a white woman responded. *"Why wouldn't black women want to trade places with us?"* Practically every other white female echoed the same bewilderment.

One African-American woman who has the appearance of a Caucasian explained:

I am asked all the time why I don't just pass for white and make things easier for myself. But I would never want to be white. I love my race.

All of my brothers and sisters have also made the decision that we would never give up our racial heritage, our darker-skinned family members, and the special qualities that make us who we are just to be white.

In the same session, women were asked if they wanted to be men. All answered in the negative. The reply given by one white female was typical:

As much as I am sometimes jealous of the benefits and power that men have just because they are men—especially white men, I would not want to change places with them. I love being a woman and having the wonderful qualities that are unique to women. I don't think I'd make a very good man, anyway—I would never want to give up my feminine quali-ties.

I do think it would be helpful to have a session dealing with the challenges of remaining feminine and proud of being a woman while moving up the corporate ladder, especially when men perceive so many typically feminine characteris-tics as negative.

In spite of the problems that prejudice and discrimination bring, white women will generally answer that they do not want to be white men. African-American men and women give the same answer.

This is not to say that women and minority men would not like to have or share power, wealth, and influence generally controlled by white people, particularly white men. It means that women and minority men are simply not willing to give up who and what they most value about themselves to do so. If these groups truly *believed* they were inferior, given the chance, it would seem that they would surely rush to trade places with white men.

REACTIONS TO BEING DEPRIVED OF ACCEPTANCE

If women and minority men do not feel inferior to white men, why then have they not handled prejudice and discrimination *from a more empowered position?* Because of prejudicial treatment, women and minority men seem to have relinquished personal power, usually without realizing it.

Might they believe that if white men were to share the positive view women and minority men have of themselves, they would accept them, and then prejudice and discrimination would end? Because humans naturally crave the things they are most deprived of, the approval of white men can be very seductive. Many women and minority men have already amassed fortunes and attained powerful positions. What they often still desire is validation as important, complete humans—validation they think must come from white men (or white people in the case of minorities).

Women and minority men must understand that their own acceptance and approval is the most essential quality for their sense of self-worth and self-esteem. This is critically important, for in their ongoing quest for approval from others, women and minority men may actually be colluding with oppression and getting farther away from the very thing they ultimately desire—a world free of prejudice and discrimination.

REACTIONS TO VICTIMIZATION

Women and minority men have responded to discriminatory treatment in a number of ways. Allport (1958) identified a variety of tactics called ego defenses, some considered socially acceptable, others, clearly not. Although these tactical behaviors are commonplace, they are most always ineffective. For example, as in the case of the two black managers with regard to their seat assignment on the airplane, people may smile and not confront a situation. No resolution there. Others may fight, argue, or seek revenge. Every type of ego defense can be found among members of any targeted group; no particular patterns identify any one.

Following is a brief summary of ego defenses that women and minority men have resorted to when treated prejudicially.

Denial of membership:

When an individual moves away from his or her group and tries to assimilate into the dominant group, this ego defense is at work—for example, passing for white to gain the benefits of the majority race. Passing is not peculiar to black people. In order to blend into the dominant White-Anglo-Saxon-Protestant group, members of other racial, ethnic, and religious groups have changed names, facial features, or religions.

Believing they can better break through the glass ceiling, some corporate women adopt stereotypically masculine styles of decision-making, leadership, dress, and communication (Cross, Katz, Miller, Seashore, Eds., 1994). One very attractive, young, white female said she deliberately played down her looks.

> *When I present myself as an attractive woman, people do not take me as seriously. Even women sometimes make comments that make me feel conspicuous if I dress up. So I just pull my hair back, and I dress like this, but I hate it. Sometimes I wish I were 40 years old so looks wouldn't matter anymore.*

(That statement has to make you smile.)

Obsessive concern or preoccupation with the problem:

Minority people constantly deal with the unpleasantness of being the only one or one of only a few in a majority world. They often feel isolated, on the defensive, and fearful that they will again be targets of discriminatory acts.

Whites in the U.S. rarely experience being a racial minority. When they do, that memory sticks with them for a long time. One white man describes how he felt being the only white person at an all-black function:

> As each minute passed, alternating feelings of intrusion and isolation began to arise. Then it dawned on me: This is how minority members must feel at most meetings.

> While that thought still lingered, a man approached and offered a brief introduction. "Welcome to the coalition," he said. Then he walked to the bar. During the next 15 minutes, six coalition members welcomed me. I was no longer the intruder breaking into a private function. Now I felt like a participant.

> As I walked to the session following the reception, I realized that if I had been a black attending a typical white meeting, chances are that no one would have made me feel welcome, even though it would have been obvious that I felt isolated (Joseph Conlin, 1989, p. 52).

Another white man recalls his experience being a minority among blacks:

> A buddy of mine who is black invited me to play basketball one evening. Little did I realize, I would be the only white person on the court.

> When I got there, I looked around and all I saw were black guys. So, I tried to nonchalantly shrug off the strangeness, act natural, and play ball.

> When I look back on it, I had a good time, but my thoughts all evening were filled with fears. What if these guys decided to jump on me? What if they tried to rough me up on the court?

> Actually, the guys were real friendly and we had a great game. But I have never quite forgotten the experience. Is this

how black people feel every day? We take it for granted that they just automatically adjust to us or that they have learned how to adapt, so it's easier for them to be around whites all the time. But is it really easier?

Withdrawal and passivity:

When using this coping mechanism, people hide behind a facade of acquiescence or contentment while on the inside they may be teeming with rage. Or they may just give up, feeling that anything they do would be futile.

A white woman gave an example of withdrawal:

I prefer to observe. I don't usually get too involved in group discussions because I really don't get the impression anyone wants to hear what I have to say.

Basically, I'm okay just listening. I think if I acted like I cared about something, people would think I was getting "too emotional." So I usually just keep pretty quiet.

Believing that what she had to say was of no particular interest to others, she cloaked her feelings in an *it-doesn't-really-matter-to-me* attitude.

A black man from the South gave another example of passivity as a coping mechanism. In his hometown, black people customarily gave up the sidewalk and meekly held their heads down when white people passed. While they hated doing this, they usually did it anyway in order to protect themselves and their families from otherwise certain harm.

Clowning:

Clowning is sometimes exhibited in patronizing, self-belittling behavior. Portraying the clown accommodates the expectations and allays the fears of others. An example would be comedians who, by making demeaning jokes about their own group, feel they are increasing their acceptability.

Clowning is also seen in the way women and minority men in television sitcoms, dramas and feature films sometimes allow themselves to be portrayed in insulting roles. It's as if by being portrayed in a lesser light, they gain the acceptance of people who see this as the behavior they would expect from these people.

Strengthening in-group ties:

Sometimes people stick with members of their own group to shield each other from isolation, to develop solidarity, and support one another. When there are only a few minority people in a majority work group, they may seek each other out for companionship.

However, such togetherness is certain to draw attention. In a cartoon, a white person encountering two black men at a coffee machine says, *"What's this... a black-power conference?"* (Floyd, 1969). Many women and minority men are often asked why they are *always* together. It may not occur to people that just as white men may prefer the association of other white men over women and minority men in the workplace, members of these groups might choose to associate with others like themselves. One black woman commented jokingly about a large group of white people in a nearly all-white audience at a stadium, *"Look, they're all sitting together again; why do they stick together like that?"*

Today, organizational in-group networking and internal advocacy groups are occurring more frequently and becoming somewhat more acceptable (Ann Morrison, 1993). Although widespread acceptance of such networks remains to be seen, support networks are being formally recognized.

Sympathy:

People who have been victims of hardship may be inclined to react sympathetically toward others who are also victims of hardship. As an example, mistrust of beggars is widespread. At a busy intersection where a crippled, seemingly homeless white man stood with a cardboard sign that read *Odd jobs for food*, one driver after another passed this man by.

Yet, a few did stop to hand the man some money. Without exception, every driver who aided him in that few minutes of observation was African-American. This is not to say that only black people help others in need. It does indicate that people who believe a beggar's situation to be legitimate—perhaps because they have experienced hard times too—may have less prejudice and suspicion.

Two homeless men, an older white man and a younger black man, stood on a downtown street. The hand of the older man was cupped to hold his few coins. He was feebly counting them, one coin at a time, to share with the younger man. This tender gesture is another example of the propensity of people to help others when they know first-hand what they may be going through.

A black female married to a white man revealed the pain she underwent being rejected by her husband's family and friends while her husband enjoyed a very warm reception among her family members and friends who were familiar with rejection first-hand.

A white female emotionally relayed the following:

> *While on a business trip, a black co-worker who had transferred to this city was having a gathering at her home. I was invited, but I knew all the other guests would be black.*
>
> *It was a very uncomfortable feeling because I was afraid these people would not accept me. As it turns out, the gathering was quite enjoyable. All the guests were nice and friendly, and they went out of their way to make me feel at home.*
>
> *Even still, I was uncomfortable since this was a completely new experience for me. I cry now when I think about blacks who are always in hostile environments, and who are always in the minority around whites who usually do nothing to try and make them feel comfortable. I don't know how they can go through this every day.*

Fighting back: Militancy:

Some refuse to accept discrimination, choosing instead, to fight back. The Civil-Rights Movement of the late 1960's is a good example of how the militancy of civil-rights activists, along with non-violent tactics, brought about landmark equal-employment legislation.

The women's movement, especially when it took a militant approach, has been instrumental in bringing women's issues to the surface and influencing positive change. Certainly, women's right to vote came only after women demanded change. The Equal Pay Act was created to guarantee that women doing the same jobs as men receive the same pay as men; however, in many cases, it took class-action lawsuits to force compliance.

Few civil rights have been won without hard-fought battles. Advocates of fighting for human rights often quote Frederick Douglass, who said, *"Power concedes nothing without a demand. It never did. It never will"* (Mann, 1991).

Enhanced striving:

This coping mechanism is reflected in the extra effort people put forth to succeed against the odds. Many of us know of situations where school counselors advised individuals to pursue low-skill vocations, yet the result was that these people only worked harder to achieve their goals and prove their advisors wrong.

Says a white-female engineer:

In high school, I was counseled to study home economics. I was always good in math and science and my parents encouraged me, even though we didn't have much money.

I knew I would have to earn a scholarship to help with my college. So I worked extra hard, actually for two reasons. One was to prove my high school counselor wrong.

But the other reason was to be able to live my dreams. I was determined and fortunate; I excelled in school and got a scholarship. It all worked out. I never understood why someone would try to convince me to settle for less than what I was capable of.

Symbolic status striving:

This is when a person shows the world that she or he has succeeded against the odds. Examples of this are seen in individuals who put their money into things intended to impress others. For instance, people may drive expensive automobiles or wear expensive jewelry to give the rest of the world a glimpse of the material success they have attained in spite of the many obstacles they faced.

Denial:

The resolution of most problems begins with recognizing there is one. This can be challenging when pain and discomfort accompany the truth. Thus, people deny their problems. Although this is a common defense, people may not recognize their actions as denial.

For example, a white-female manager at a diversity-training session made the following comment:

> Everyone says that white women are passive and unassertive, but that's not true. It's not that we are passive. We just know how to get what we want.
>
> We know that if we act too aggressive, men will be turned off, so we sometimes have to pretend to go along with something, when really, we're not.
>
> But in the end, we get what we want. I believe that is being assertive.

This woman may not have felt she was denying the problem, but her comment reflects how people can explain away rather than see a difficult situation for what it is. Certainly, people hearing her comment did not think her assertive, but rather saw her as passive, shrewd, and manipulative.

It is impossible to grow up free from the effects of prejudice and discrimination. Yet, many people do not recognize them when they see them. So, I will repeat: only when we acknowledge that problems exist will we be compelled to do something about them.

Aggression against own group:

Using this mechanism, when people are treated as if they have no worth, they may act out on others in their group the very prejudice inflicted on them.

A Mexican-American woman gave an example. She described a divisive class system among Hispanics: Hispanics sharing similar lifestyles and physical characteristics with Caucasians looking down on those from different Spanish-speaking cultures, especially ones who spoke little or no English or who spoke English with a heavy accent. Thus, not only did they face discrimination from Caucasians, they faced it from other Hispanics.

Resignation:

Resignation occurs when a person is no longer willing or able to ward off negative messages and succumbs to hopelessness. A film entitled The *Pike Syndrome* (Ramic Productions, 1987) powerfully depicts this phenomenon.

In this film, a large pike is placed in a glass tank. Tiny minnows are separated from the fish by a large, clear, glass jar. Repeatedly, as the pike lunges forward to catch a minnow, it strikes its head against the glass that separates it from its meal.

After a time, it tries less and less. Finally, the glass is removed, but by now the fish, weakened from hunger and conditioned to receiving a painful blow whenever it tried to eat, has given up. The minnows swim freely around the tank. The large fish dies from starvation.

Allport addresses this syndrome poignantly:

> *Ask yourself what would happen to your own personality if you heard it said over and over again that you were lazy, a simple child of nature, expected to steal, and had inferior blood. Suppose this opinion were forced on you by the majority of your fellow citizens. And suppose nothing that you could do would change this opinion...*

One's reputation, whether false or true, cannot be hammered, hammered, hammered, into one's head without doing something to one's character (1958, p. 139).

As women at a seminar listened to the national news reporting on the white man (mentioned in a previous chapter) who had murdered his wife and blamed a black man, U.S. black women listened quietly. The white women did the same. However, a black woman from Jamaica erupted, "Why do they do these terrible things and try to blame black people? This is sickening; I can't stand it! When is it going to stop...?"

Of this incident, one of the American black women explained,

From this woman's reaction, I realized just how quiet and accepting we seemed to be about such horrendous news. It took the woman from Jamaica to vocalize what we probably all felt. I really admired her freedom to speak without inhibition, no matter who was in the room.

We (U.S. black women) are probably so accustomed to bad news, and we are also programmed to not reacting in mixed company. It may even be because we didn't want to make the white women uncomfortable by saying anything. But I can see now that such silence comes across as passive acceptance.

DEALING WITH THE PROBLEM FROM AN EMPOWERED POSITION

Certainly, most of the coping responses described above have failed to produce lasting change. Women and minority men must develop a different strategy, one that will lead to sustained improvement. Here are some things they can do:

- **Start by creating a mental picture of the ideal diverse workforce.**

They must aim high and ask, *"If human conditions were as good as they could possibly be, what would things look like?"* The answer provides momentum to drive out the quick-fix, low-impact ego defenses that change nothing or result only in short-term improvement.

- **Make correcting problems a joint effort that includes white men.**

  Take responsibility and do not accept the status quo. Seek ways to become more effective—replacing low-impact behavior with constructive, empowered actions that produce long-term systemic success. (This will not be easy since behavior is learned and reinforced over lifetimes.) Learn to define and describe the conditions of racism and sexism in ways that cause leadership to listen and become committed to eradicating them.

- **Make a critical self-appraisal of skills and capabilities.**

  Women and minority men must realize that, just as every white male does not make it to the top, when discrimination is eliminated, neither will every woman or minority man. However, in a prejudice-and-discrimination-free environment, they will no longer have to wonder if they did not succeed because of race or gender.

- **Seek greater self-awareness and re-assess priorities.**

  Women and minority men must examine their view of themselves and their race and/or sex and learn to value the perception they have of themselves. They should ask: *"Does someone else's opinion matter more than my own or members of my race or gender?" "Do I feel that someone else's acceptance is more important than self acceptance?"* Self-validation rather than the fleeting approval of the dominant group is the aim.

- **Remember the self-fulfilling prophecy—you get what you expect.**

  Set high expectations, be deliberate and strategic, and do not compromise by complying with the limited expectations of others. They must expect much from themselves and deliver accordingly.

CONCLUSION

The road to full diversity is not for white males only. Just as everyone should be involved in helping to create the desired culture, there must be shared responsibility and ownership for addressing and correcting the problems.

The intent of this chapter has been to highlight the role of women and minority men in ensuring progress, and to offer insights into dealing more effectively with the problems of prejudice and discrimination in the workplace.

By understanding the possible impact of the self-fulfilling prophecy, common ego defenses, and internalized oppression on self-image, women and minority men can see how their reactions to prejudice and discrimination may have served to enable rather than to correct problems.

To be most effective, women and minority men must assume an empowered position, know the problem, and be able to articulate it in a way that prompts others to action. Finally, they must hold organizational leadership accountable and expect them to be responsive.

"No one can make you feel inferior without your consent."

Eleanor Roosevelt
This is My Story (1937)

•NINE•

A PREJUDICE AND DISCRIMINATION-FREE WORKPLACE

It should be assumed that all employees want to succeed and are capable of doing so, and treated accordingly.

Organizational leaders sometimes embrace the newest management concepts—quality programs, restructuring, re-engineering—fully expecting them to bring success and profitability to their operations. So far, none have been completely successful. Still, leaders have not yet jumped at the chance to advance diversity which has tremendous potential to bring long-term success and profitability.

But managing diversity, unlike some initiatives, is not a passing fancy. It is a smart, long-term business strategy. By creating highly productive work forces, leaders help businesses operate competitively and attain their goals. Effective diversity management can make the substantial difference for today's organizations.

When senior leaders make the decision to embark on this challenging endeavor, they must treat it as they would any other major change initiative—by putting resources, goals and timetables together, holding the organization accountable and implementing a system to measure success. And, as with any major initiative, they would do well to solicit the input of the women and men of the organization. When they do, they might find shocking the sentiments expressed. Listen, for example, to a key, white-female manager in corporate America.

> *I'm scared for this company. I feel we are cycling backward. Increasingly I see this, especially when I look at the men who continue to get promoted to higher levels.*

It shows me that our management just does not get it yet. Diversity is treated like it is on the back burner, or as something we already did. It's definitely not something ongoing.

This woman went on to say:

I have been told that I'm about to be reassigned to work for a man I worked for once before. This man was a male-chauvinist pig. But he keeps going up the ladder of success. Before, I told his boss I could not work for him any longer, so I was reassigned to someone else.

I thought they were being responsive, but now I am about to be assigned to the same man again. And he hasn't changed. I guess that's their way of showing me what they think of me.

I haven't told them yet, but I am now pregnant, and when I go on maternity leave, I won't be coming back. A number of other companies are seeking my abilities, talents and experience. I'll go where I can feel valued.

It probably did come as a surprise to her management when she resigned to *pursue other interests*. There are undoubtedly as many stories like hers as there are women and minority men in organizations. People are hired. Some stay and are productive; others stay but are underutilized. Many leave for reasons that have to do with diversity issues. New people are hired and the cycle continues ad infinitum unless organizations take the initiative to break that cycle and move forward.

EXECUTIVE COMMITMENT TO DIVERSITY

Prejudice and discrimination are often institutionalized through internal customs, policies, and operating practices. The remedy—a renewal of organizational systems—is largely in the hands of organizational leaders (King, 1981).

It may be difficult for senior leaders to accept this responsibility. It is common to hear executives say, *"I had no idea this was happening in our organization; I thought we were doing fine."* Ignorance, though, is no longer an excuse.

In some cases, diversity training has helped to enlighten employees. Often, however, top management in those companies does not participate in this training. Some may feel they do not need it. Or, perhaps, they went through diversity training years ago. They may think that offering the program to their employees addresses issues adequately and demonstrates that diversity is a priority. But diversity training can be helpful for people at all levels, and even more so for those who influence organizational culture.

Cultural anthropologist, Steve Barnett (1986), cites statements by corporate executives that indicate a need for cultural-diversity awareness at that level. One CEO whose company had just committed to a minority-hiring program relayed his ambivalence to Mr. Barnett. *"Tell me, are blacks really as smart as we are? I've never seen it" (p.48).* Barnett continues:

> *Another CEO repeatedly referred to his black customers at a company strategy meeting as "members of tribes who were becoming restless." At a third company meeting, a vice-president used the word "nigger." And this by an ad agency account executive: "A little rhythm and blues, a tight dress and the jigs are sold."*

Should we consider Barnett's examples out-of-date because *things are different now?* Or, do we need to be reminded of the *black-jelly-bean* incident of 1996 (Roberts, 1998), to realize that the more things change, the more they remain the same. Rather than the exception, Barnett could be citing the norm. Isolated or commonplace, spoken within earshot of others or not, these comments should not be made.

If top managers are prejudiced, it becomes acceptable for employees to be prejudiced too. If managers have never taken the time to become knowledgeable about diversity issues, they diminish, if not negate, the effectiveness of diversity efforts.

It is possible for well-meaning senior officials to be completely out of touch with the day-to-day experiences of lower-level employees. These managers may issue statements espousing company support of diversity and expect employees to comply with their edicts.

They may hear from advisors (who may or may not see the entire picture) that all is well. (Many civil-rights lawsuits appeared at a time leadership thought everything was going well.) Therefore, before senior leaders champion diversity, they should conduct an honest self-appraisal, asking themselves, *"Is it possible that I may be guilty of overt or covert discrimination?"* (Many people adamantly believe they do not discriminate against others. However, it does not matter from what walk of life or economic strata people come, if they grew up in the U.S., they will have learned stereotyping and prejudice. These ideologies do not automatically evaporate as senior managers climb the corporate ladder.)

Senior leaders must work to eliminate their own stereotypical thinking and prejudices. Here, personal advisors—people off whom they can bounce ideas, debate or ask questions without being judged adversely, and who will give sound counsel—can be invaluable. It should not be assumed that every woman or minority man can perform the role of personal advisor. Many may still be learning how to think about, articulate, and effectively handle diversity issues themselves. Or they may not want the role. (To those individuals who have the opportunity to be an advisor, know that senior managers do not need *yes* people. Rather, they need someone they can look to for straight talk, who will challenge their thinking, and provide important insights.)

SOMETHING IS WRONG WITH THIS PICTURE

The most visible measure of an organization's commitment to diversity is reflected in the makeup of the work force across the organization. Thus, senior managers should take a close look at their organizations from top to bottom. If all things are equal and racism and sexism are absent, women of all races and minority men will be proportionately represented. If the majority of women and minority men are concentrated at lower levels and across only certain parts of the organization, senior managers should immediately conclude that something is wrong.

Historically, it has taken approximately twenty years to move from entry to top levels (Hyman, 1981). Naturally, not everyone moves up the ladder, as organizations are not generally structured to allow all employees to do so. Neither are all employees equally qualified to operate across all levels and functions.

Those who traditionally make it to the top have been white men while women of all races and minority men are stalled in the low to mid-levels where many remain for the duration of their careers (Braham, 1987). Sometimes they quit in frustration. On the other hand, when systems support the development of all employees, all groups of people move up at about the same pace. Hypothetically, if women comprise a certain percent of managers and have been in the organization long enough, all things being equal, they should hold at least that same percent of top management positions.

Obviously, at higher corporate levels, the numbers of women and minority men are not at all reflective of their representation in organizations. (Neither is their presence in organizations typically reflective of their numbers in the general population.) A 1980's survey showed blacks accounting for less than one percent of senior executives (Braham, 1987). And although women comprised nearly half of the U.S. work force and two-thirds of new work force entrants, they held only a fraction of top positions in Fortune 1000 firms.

A decade later, only five percent of all Fortune 500 corporate board members were women. Fewer than six were chief executives (Winikow, 1991). As we embark on the 21st Century, the numbers have changed little. With the departure of Jill Barad from Mattel in early 2000, only three women remain as CEO's of Fortune 500 companies (NPR, Feb. 4, 2000). In a discrimination-free work world, if they make up 50 percent of the work force, the number of women at the level of chief executive officer in Fortune 1,000 firms should be closer to 500!

Top managers might rationalize the slow advancement up the corporate ladder as the *best to be expected* from individuals stereotypically considered deficient or inadequate. If so, this suggests prejudice.

Looking at another side of the picture, some women and minority men have held premium jobs that typically lead to higher levels. Some have even succeeded, yet, many have not. One reason some have not succeeded has been the existence of a hostile work environment. A young woman manager in a non-traditional role describes such an environment:

> *My department operated around the clock. Whenever I was on call as the troubleshooter, rarely did I sleep through an entire night uninterrupted. The guys in my department made it a point to call me every night, sometimes several times a night, often for decisions that they were perfectly capable of making themselves.*
>
> *It was unending. They made my life miserable, and I often wondered if it was worth it. I managed to hang in there, but it never got any better while I was in that particular role.*

Senior management should be questioning why this low level of progression is occurring. To get at the root of the problem, they should ask:

- Why would I not expect to see women of all races and minority men working at all levels and across every part of the organization?

- Could my expectations possibly be influenced by stereotypical beliefs?

- Have I ever even wondered why I see so few black women reaching higher levels? How can it be that people who were highly qualified when they were hired suddenly became mediocre or inadequate when they are placed in competition with white males?

- Am I satisfied with the current situation? Why or why not? Have I done everything I could to ensure that women and minority men are not being set up for failure?

Improvement will come, in part, when managers at all levels

view the work force distribution imbalance as their problem, not as a battle to be waged solely by women and minority men.

Getting To the Root Of The Problem

"You're not quite ready for promotion;" "You need just one more assignment;" "You need just a little more experience;" "You need to demonstrate more leadership." Many woman and minority men have heard these dreaded words that substantiate their fears that the rules of promotion are different for them than for white men.

Across U.S. workplaces, evidence suggests that promotions are influenced by race or gender (Olson & Frieze, 1987). Research has found that women of all races are held to higher promotion standards than men and receive fewer promotions than men with whom they are equally qualified (Olson and Becker, 1983). Blacks also have lower rates of promotion than whites in the same organizations (Greenhaus, Parasuraman, and Wormely, 1990).

People who make promotion decisions may feel they are being thorough by considering all aspects of readiness of women or minority men, including all possible *what if*'s. However, many woman and minority men believe that white-male candidates are given the benefit of the doubt.

A white woman learned she was not offered a promotion for reasons that probably do not usually affect male colleagues.

> *It was well after the fact that I learned my name had been submitted for a promotion that involved a transfer to another city. I never knew about this at the time, but it turns out, my managers made the decision for me. They felt that since I was married, I would not want to move. After all, what about my husband's job?*

> *You know, I may not have wanted to transfer, but I should have been given the chance to turn it down rather than to have others make the decision for me. This was very upsetting.*

Just as in the performance-rating process, top management ought to participate in staffing meetings so they can hear the promotion discussions first-hand. When they conclude it is primarily women and minority men who are perpetually not quite ready for promotion, leaders should again ask, *"What's really going on here?"* and insist on straight answers.

One senior official committed to diversity shared how he addressed the *not-quite-ready-for-promotion* syndrome. Year after year, as his top managers made promotion decisions for higher-level positions, the women and minority men on the list were invariably *twelve months away from promotion readiness*. The following year, they would still be still twelve months away. Frustrated, this manager informed his leadership that unless they had very good reasons for not promoting these people in the upcoming twelve months, he expected them to be promoted. Overnight, promotions started happening.

This is a good example of how top management can make strategic interventions. However, this method was reactionary and did not create an ongoing system to sustain improvement. The man has retired and it is not known whether his fairness has continued. Progress must not hinge on an individual. To be successful, all organizational members must manage by the same principles. Then, it will not matter who the key decision makers are.

Watts and Carter (1991) state that efforts at ending institutional racism and sexism have emphasized hiring, promotion, seniority, remuneration, and working conditions. But, focusing on these limited areas is not sufficient to address the pervasive nature of institutional *isms*.

So, how do we get to the heart of the problem? By addressing the organizational culture, says Grover Hankins (1997):

> *Many organizations feel they are dealing with diversity when they find the one or two blatant perpetrators of discriminatory practices and announce that these people will have to attend diversity-awareness classes.*

Or, they single out the one department that has had a known infraction, and set up procedures to "fix" members of that department...

Organization leaders sometimes think the problem is limited to just a few players rather than accepting that diversity problems usually reflect the entire organizational culture. In reality, it is the entire organization that needs "fixing."

IMPLICATIONS OF DIVERSITY MANAGEMENT

No matter how profitable, few organizations can treat lightly substantial losses to their bottom line. A study by Cox and Blake (1991) showed that properly managing cultural diversity could provide a competitive advantage across multiple areas including costs, resource acquisitions, and problem solving.

Costs:

Turnover of women and minority men resulting from low job satisfaction, frustration over career growth, cultural conflict, even termination for cause, is often the result of diversity mismanagement and may represent a significant percent of turnover costs. Diversity efforts resulting in increased employee utilization and productivity could translate into additional savings.

Human-Resource Acquisition:

Companies generally seek to attract and retain the best employees. A prevalent pattern has been that female and minority male recruits qualified because of their GPA's and demonstrated leadership are highly sought after. Often, however, these new hires enter a workplace that is not prepared to accept them as successful contributors. After a time, they become classified as moderate performers (Jones, 1986), and, within a few years, many leave to *pursue other interests.*

Meanwhile, without attempting to create the prejudice-and-discrimination-free environments conducive to success, organizations continue recruiting the best and the brightest women and minority men only to see them leave a few years later. *"They just can't cut it around here,"* some muse resignedly. Sadly, the new entrants leave just as the next wave enters, and the cycle continues.

Creativity in Problem Solving:

As heterogeneous groups tend to approach problem solving from a richer base of options, minority viewpoints on organizational teams are good for business. Research by Charlene Nemeth (1986) found that minorities stimulated more consideration of non-obvious alternatives, while Cox and Blake (1991) found that if people from diverse gender, nationality, racial, and ethnic groups have different perspectives on issues, they increased their teams' creativity and innovation.

BENCHMARKING IN MANAGING CULTURAL DIVERSITY

Some leaders, seeking ways to improve their diversity management systems use benchmarking. As it gives organizations a gauge to measure progress, benchmarking can effectively establish baseline data and operating parameters as well as set goals and targets.

Yet, while it may be helpful to know what other organizations are doing, in the critical area of diversity management, the company that measures its progress against others may be setting its sights too low since most organizations have plenty of room for growth. For example, few, if any, companies have placed an equitable number of women and minority men in executive positions.

Klemmerer and Arnold (1993) identified the absence of cultural bias, prejudice, and discrimination as indicative of a true multi-cultural organization. Have any companies been completely successful in eliminating prejudice and discrimination? It is doubtful.

Sometimes women and minority men who work for companies cited as the best companies to work for say, *"If our company is one of the best, I would hate to see the worst. We still have a very long way to go.*" Thus, organizations must not use the limited progress of other companies as a reason to forego setting aggressive goals. The company that takes the brave stance of working to eliminate prejudice and discrimination will signal itself a leader. As other companies seek to emulate it, that company has the potential to gain a competitive advantage.

Diversity-Training Programs

Diversity training has become a popular component of many employee-development and cultural-diversity efforts. Estimates suggest as many as one-third of America's largest corporations offer some kind of diversity training to employees (NPR, 1994).

In a 1991 study, Towers Perrin found that 75 percent of surveyed companies either had diversity-training programs in place or planned to offer them. For example, all 12,000 mid-to-upper-level managers at a large insurance company had completed a two-day training. This program was then introduced to the rest of the company's 100,000 employees (Caudron, 1993).

The success of diversity training programs and their benefit to organizations may be difficult to ascertain. Workshop training, even if experiential, is not usually as long lasting as desired, and applying the teachings after the training can be difficult. If its purpose is clear, objectives met, and principle-based management and other reminders of the organization's commitment to diversity constantly support it, the effects of diversity workshops can be long lasting.

Morris Massey (1986) says it takes a *significant emotional event* for people to change core beliefs, values, attitudes, and behaviors. It may be unrealistic to expect a two or three-day workshop to be that event. While such training may be helpful, it is a challenge to influence individual attitudes and behavior for the long term.

Yet, well-designed and executed diversity training can be effective, possibly even life-transforming. Obviously, life transformation is not easy to accomplish. Prejudicial walls must be broken down and relationships rebuilt based on valuing individual differences. The training must also provide insightful information while not polarizing or alienating diverse groups.

Even the most successful diversity training can, at best, only begin to tackle the task. This is why an organization's diversity strategy must include more than training programs. The organization must reinforce daily that it values diversity in order to create the environment in which awareness and insights gained through training can positively influence how people interact.

The matter of trainers and consultants must be discussed briefly. According to York (1994, pp. 119-121), almost anyone who wants to be a cross-cultural trainer can find work. Unfortunately, few programs prepare diversity trainers to deliver transforming results. Thus, quality and effectiveness vary widely. It is critical that leaders insist on trainers capable of delivering results. In-house trainers can sometimes be as effective as outside professionals.

Senior managers are urged to participate in all aspects of diversity management, including selecting and participating in training programs. They will benefit from knowing what the rest of the organization is learning. While authorizing the company's diversity-management program is one thing; showing up personally is another. By leading the charge, top managers show they are serious and expect others to be as well.

PART OF THE SOLUTION OR PART OF THE PROBLEM

Although it can be relatively easy to dismiss diversity issues as someone else's problem and thus do nothing, all people play a part directly or indirectly in perpetuating prejudice and discrimination. Equally important, they must play a part in eliminating them.

An exercise sometimes used in diversity training helps participants see this. A grid is divided into four main blocks. Participants are asked to mentally place themselves in one of the four (active racist/sexist, active non-racist/sexist, passive racist/sexist, or passive non-racist/sexist). As they do, they must decide what these categories mean for themselves.

The responsibility grid is shown on the next page.

The Responsibility Grid		
	Racist/Sexist	Non-Racist/Sexist
Active		
Passive		

Most will place themselves in the passive non-racist/sexist block since, for the most part, people who are not outright, blatantly prejudiced usually see themselves as harmless observers of these problems. This exercise helps them reconsider.

Next, participants are asked to give examples for each group. For the active racist/sexist block they might say such things as, member of white-supremacy groups, against women's rights, practices segregation from other race/gender, or tells ethnic/gender jokes.

Conversely, the passive racist/sexist might be described as someone who secretly condones activities of white-supremacy groups, tacitly approves of discrimination against women and minority men, or laughs (or does nothing) when ethnic/gender jokes are told.

Active non-racist/sexists will likely be identified as people who confront racist and sexist policies and behavior, challenge people who tell derogatory jokes, teach others including their children not to be prejudiced.

Even though the passive/*non*-racist/sexist block is the one in which most people will have placed themselves at the beginning, they have great difficulty describing it. Much to their surprise, everything suggested is more appropriate for the passive racist/sexist block. No matter how hard they brainstorm, they cannot come up with good examples. Invariably, someone says, *"I don't think there can be a passive non-racist/sexist."* He or she is correct.

Even though they had considered themselves harmlessly non-involved, participants see that by their do-nothing behavior they are actually being passive racists/sexists. This is a painful but powerful realization. Said one woman, *"How passive I have become! I am ashamed of how complacent I have become to my own issues and those of others."*

The exercise delivers a potent message: everyone—women of all races, minority men, and white men—owns a part of addressing the serious problems of prejudice and discrimination. As this is the case, they have an obligation *and* a right to do something. Those not actively participating in solutions are part of the problem. As one participant put it: *"Doing nothing about racism and sexism is worse than being an active racist or sexist."*

When a white female participant explained she felt hurt that she could not invite her black female friend to visit her small town because it was a very racist town, a black woman responded:

> *I understand and appreciate how you feel. But, what are you doing about the problem? You should know that it is not enough just to be hurt by the problem. Something has to be done about it.*
>
> *As long as you do nothing, you give the racists your permission to exist. By your inactivity, you are essentially giving the perpetrators your tacit approval, even condoning their actions.*
>
> *People should not be able to enjoy complete freedom to do whatever they want, regardless of whom they hurt. Harmful racist behaviors must be met with some consequences—some conscious expressions of disapproval.*
>
> *I know it's very hard to confront others; it is hard for me. But we need to start taking a stand and letting people know that hurting others is just not okay.*

A paper entitled "Becoming Antiracist/Racists" cited only two ways that whites can behave. One is as racists—those who

gain the benefits of being white and consciously or unconsciously support institutional and cultural practices that perpetuate racism. The other is as antiracists—recipients of these
privileges who recognize they are illegitimately obtained
because of skin color, but strive to remove them (National
Education Association, 1973). Change a few words and the
same definition can be used to describe sexists or anti-sexists.

The paper concludes:

> *It is not hard to be racist/racists, especially when we have
> been born and raised in a society that fostered white racism
> and condones and supports it.*

> *It is very hard to be antiracist/racists—whites who work
> directly and actively against racism in all its forms. But if we
> as whites are serious, there is no alternative.*

If people shirk their responsibility to eradicate racism and sexism, these negative forces will forever remain a part of the organizational culture.

CONCLUSION

Diversity efforts and practices such as benchmarking or training
programs may not automatically deliver successful results. This is
especially so if they are implemented without leaders first preparing the organization by insisting on a prejudice-and-discrimination-free environment.

If organizational leaders know of prejudice and discriminatory
treatment, they must take the necessary steps to eliminate it. A
principle-based approach is the most effective way to achieve lasting results.

Specific steps organizational leaders can take will be discussed
in the next and final chapter.

"Come, come, my conservative friend.
Wipe the dew off your spectacles,
and see that the world is moving."

Elizabeth Cady Stanton
From Part I of *The Woman's Bible* (1895)

TEN

THE ROLE OF SENIOR MANAGERS

*If people have the right information, and believe it
to be true, they will generally be moved to action*

enior managers run their organizations to promote the best
interests of all stakeholders—owners, employees, community,
government, suppliers, customers, and consumers. In this
regard, they zealously protect and exercise their responsibilities and
rights. Moreover, they fully expect all employees to embrace company philosophies, values, policies, and principles. However, when
it comes to cultural diversity, they seem to abdicate their authority.

If they address diversity at all, they may assign a diversity manager or affirmative-action officer, usually a woman or minority man.
Very often, this person has little preparation or authority. Or,
instead of assuming responsibility for creating prejudice-and-discrimination-free work environments, they symbolically throw up
their hands from not knowing how, or even whether to try and
influence employee attitudes and behaviors.

CHANGING THE ORGANIZATION'S CULTURE

The role of leaders, as explained by Kotter (1996), is to define
what the future should look like, align people to that vision and,
even in the face of obstacles, inspire them to reach it. Regarding
diversity, leaders must make clear that the vision of achieving full
diversity in a prejudice- and discrimination-free workplace is not
optional.

Those with authority can best demonstrate how employees
should act. If senior people can influence behavior relative to other
work force policies and practices, they can do so with diversity
management. By visibly role-modeling, by communicating clear
expectations, and by exacting rewards and consequences for behavior, senior managers control the levers that determine the careers,

pay, promotability, and, ultimately, the behavior and thinking of their work force.

As many change efforts fail, it is quite probable that leaders do not automatically know appropriate techniques and strategies. There are resources. Sometimes, human-resource personnel or outside consultants may be skilled in the change process. Abundant literature is also available. Leaders are advised to avail themselves of resources as needed to ensure efforts to achieve full diversity are successful and long lasting.

COMPONENTS OF GOOD DIVERSITY MANAGEMENT

Leaders compelled to action should consider the following elements in developing a comprehensive diversity-management strategy.

Leadership commitment and involvement:

Major organizational change is probably impossible without the support and active involvement of the hierarchy. People at lower levels take their cues from the top. The involvement of executive and senior-level managers sends an important message. If senior managers set themselves apart from the process, they convey to the rest of the organization that diversity is not a priority.

Direction setting:

Senior managers set direction for their organizations; thus, they must have a vision and be dedicated to fulfilling it. Direction setting includes clarifying the purpose of the diversity-management effort; clearly communicating expectations; and developing goals, objectives, timetables, action plans, evaluation procedures, and a system of rewards. With clear direction, the diversity effort will be treated as serious business and progress assured.

Strategic action plan:

These are specific steps that lend themselves to achieving the company's goals. For example, if one goal is to increase the rate of promotion for women and minority men, an action step might be to develop a list of potential candidates and to monitor their progress. Another step could be to establish a mentoring program, or, less formally, routine one-on-one discussions with employees. This, or any other strategic action, must be implemented with the same thoroughness as any other business goal.

Accountability and responsibility:

Some organizations' philosophy seems to be *victim, heal thyself*. Women and minority men are expected to resolve problems with prejudice and discrimination while continuing to perform business as usual. Prejudice and discrimination are tolerated, and managers are not held responsible.

Certainly, those in key positions must be made accountable. If there is no accountability, more than likely, there will be no progress. There must be clear expectations that people treat diversity issues as they would other business issues and that everyone work toward success. Individuals who place a high priority on managing diversity should be rewarded for successful results just as they are rewarded for other business success. And they should be held accountable for failure.

A system of measurement:

The organization must have a way to determine the efficacy of its efforts. The effects of diversity programs in eliminating prejudice and discrimination may be difficult to track, but leaders must find ways. Diversity efforts involving recruitment, training and development, promotion, turnover rates, and individual performance ratings should be easier to measure. Tracking, then studying, the impact of diversity efforts will aid senior managers in identifying underlying causes of problems and determining if efforts are working.

An assessment process:

Getting people to open up about a topic as serious as human differences is difficult. Therefore, enlisting experts to design and execute the right assessment tools may be appropriate.

The problem with many assessments is that they may not adequately measure whether real progress is being made. Among other things, a good diversity-assessment process will answer the following:

- Are strategies delivering the desired results?

- Are the goals of the diversity-management process being reached?

- Are the organization's results showing the expected improvement?

- Do employees recognize the change?

- What is working?

- Are prejudice and discrimination being addressed?

- How are employees feeling about the organization's diversity culture?

Armed with answers to questions like these, leaders will know whether they should continue or alter their processes to obtain better results.

The actual execution of each component will involve multiple steps. As every organization is different, these elements may or may not represent an organization's total effort. However, they represent the more fundamental elements.

GETTING STARTED

Senior managers often ask, *"Where do I go from here? What do I do? How do I get started?"* Following are ways leaders can begin implementing a diversity-management strategy. Addressed to senior organizational leaders, these recommendations can form the foundation of a solid diversity intervention sure to make a significant difference. These steps may not constitute the totality of efforts but they do offer solid direction for getting started.

- **Decide.** Deciding to get started is probably the toughest step in the entire process, and the most important one. Remember, however, that until you truly believe problems are real, you will not be compelled to act. But, when you decide to move forward, you will start to see progress across your organization.

- **Develop a vision.** Ask yourself how things would look if your organization were free from prejudice and discrimination. Think in terms of your organization's overall capacity, output, productivity levels, resource utilization, turnover, image, and culture.

- **Investigate.** Talk with organizational members, either in one-on-one sessions, focus groups, or discussion meetings to find out whether they feel your corporation is one in which all employees are free to contribute their best. Be responsive to relevant, honest feedback.

- **Examine the distribution of women and minority men.** If they are concentrated at the lower levels and/or only in limited areas, determine why. Participate in staffing meetings and learn why women and minority men take longer to move up than white men. Hear reasons why women and minority men are *not quite ready for promotion*. If there is not a very good reason, develop and deploy appropriate corrective measures.

- **Examine the salaries of employees by group.** Compare how women and minority men are paid relative to white men. If you find that their salaries on average are less than the salaries of white men otherwise equal in job level, years' service, and other criteria used by your organization, develop a plan to equalize salaries across groups. Or, if there is a range by job level, determine if women and minority men are routinely paid at the low end. If they are, study reasons to see what patterns emerge. You will probably notice the same rationale for women and minority men being recycled repeatedly. If the reasons are sound, then, of course, factor them into salary

decisions. But remember, the same salary-planning logic
should be applied to all salary decisions, including those for
white men.

- **Compare performance data.** Examine performance ratings
  of women and minority men. If data show theirs to be generally lower than white men's, examine why. Obviously, they
  were once considered highly qualified or they would not have
  been hired. Review the validity of your performance-appraisal
  and ratings processes. If the data show the performance of
  women and minority men about equal with white men, determine why these groups are not getting promoted at levels at
  par with white men. Be open to the probability that prejudice
  and discrimination are factors and prepare to deal with these
  factors. If, in the end, you find that any member of the work
  force is exercising bias toward certain groups, take appropriate steps to deal with that person. Institute a system that will
  ensure that all employees are evaluated fairly.

- **Look at the turnover rate for women and minority men**
  and compare it to the rate for white men. Examine the real
  reasons women and minority men leave your organization. As
  people sometimes believe that being honest may burn
  bridges, do not assume you are getting complete answers in
  exit interviews. Strive to build trusting relationships with all
  groups and communicate that disparate turnover rates are not
  acceptable. Develop ways to deal with managers who have a
  pattern of failure managing women and minority men and
  establish remedies. Know that for every person who leaves, it
  costs your organization anywhere from $20,000 to over
  $100,000! Multiply that by the overall turnover numbers and
  you will probably be astounded at the costs of *preventable*
  attrition.

- **Develop a set of principles** by which to guide diversity
  efforts. Introduce these principles into your organization in a
  way that all people will embrace and commit to them.

- **Establish, practice and clearly communicate a policy of non-discrimination.** Require other senior managers to comply with all facets of this policy and advise all employees that they, too, must strictly adhere to it in all aspects of the business. Hold people accountable and mete out stiff consequences if violations occur

- **Stop excluding black and other minority women** with the expression *women and minorities*. Locate the *invisible* minority females in your organization and investigate the reasons why these women have either not contributed at the same rate as others or have not received recognition for their contributions. Again, deal appropriately with managers responsible for the development of these women and institute remedies.

- **Recognize and reward women and minority men for their contributions** through promotions and salaries commensurate with white men. Bring the accomplishments of women and minority men out in the open. Probably every woman or minority man has been approached by someone who whispered, *"Hey, that was a good job."* Stop treating their accomplishments as well-guarded secrets. Also recognize individuals doing effective jobs managing employees, and again, put consequences in place for those who do not.

- **Know why you are offering diversity training and be very clear about its objectives, expectations and intent.** Sometimes training is done just because other organizations are doing it or it seems like the thing to do—not sufficient reasons to make such a major investment. If you invest in training, determine to whom it is directed and expected outcomes, then personally select the trainers and ensure they can fulfill your expectations. Hold your organization accountable for ensuring that the outcome is not short-lived. Use focus-group meetings, important one-on-one discussions, employee surveys, and regular reviews with the women and minority men in your organization to continue discussing the organization's diversity goals and objectives.

- **Be careful with quotas.** The problem with quotas is that once you have reached them, it does not matter how qualified or ready other women and minority men are, there is no more room. Also, quotas can pit one group against another, engendering competition not conducive to maximizing organizational effectiveness. If quotas are to be used, one way to think of them is as the minimum acceptable number. That way you are not restricting the opportunity for advancement to qualified others.

- **Replace words with action.** At some time or other, you will be called upon to give a diversity talk. You will undoubtedly say things like:

  - Employees are our most valuable assets. Managing diversity is our competitive advantage.

  - Women and minorities bring a new way of thinking and creativity to our organization. Cultural diversity makes us a far better company. When we have diversity, we create better products.

  - We must value and leverage the difference all of us bring.

The thing to know about these talks is that everyone has heard them repeatedly, but they have not always seen actions to back them up. The words sound politically correct, but may come across as giving shallow lip service to a serious issue.

It is time for action. Begin treating your diversity initiative as an ongoing process, not a single intervention or a speech. Aim high and insist on results. When you see the need, challenge yourself to confront your peers. Then when you are again called upon to make a presentation, you will be able to present fresh, sincere, exciting words filled with enthusiasm, spirit, and backed by results.

After acting on the above recommendations, develop a strtategy for improvement. This strategy should flow easily and naturally. Or, consider acquiring an outside or internal expert to help develop your plan.

TELL ME WHAT YOU WANT ME TO DO

"I hate it," said a white woman manager, *"when someone says, 'just tell me what you want me to do?'"* In the context of prejudice and discrimination, these words may represent earnest naiveté, or they may indicate a lack of commitment, interest, or concern. People who wish to remain detached from a problem do not try to figure out solutions. Instead, they act only when someone asks them to, and not a minute before. Continues this manager:

> *It makes me wonder why would you ask me to spell it out when you can see what's going on as clearly as I can. Besides, if I knew everything that needed to be done, I probably would not need help anyway.*
>
> *Maybe people are just wanting to know if I want them to get involved in the first place, but some things just go without saying, don't they?*
>
> *I mean if I were drowning, would someone ask me what I wanted them to do? I don't think so. To be honest, sometimes it almost feels like I am drowning.*

Very clearly, people committed to managing diversity effectively will be internally directed to act. They will not abdicate responsibility and, in case the action they take does not work, let themselves off the hook by saying, *"I only did exactly what you asked me to do."*

BEING BLIND AND DEAF TO DIFFERENCES

In corporate America, a white-female colleague happily shared that her young son proudly went to a school Halloween party dressed as M. C. Hammer, an African-American popular singer and rap artist. This mother felt proud that, in today's world, role models come in all types and colors. She found it especially gratifying that her son's young mind was not filled with negative preconceived notions about other races, that he valued people without regard to race.

On another occasion, a white woman colleague expressed jubilation that her young son also had not been tainted with prejudice. Her words said it well:

> *My children were vying for which of the Power Rangers to be, and my five-year-old son decided he wanted to be the best and toughest ranger of them all. So he chose The Black Ranger.*

> *The Black Ranger! I felt so proud of him at that moment. I felt that I had really succeeded in teaching him what is truly important. It was as if my child was somehow blind and deaf to racial differences. I wish that we could all be blind and deaf to differences that are unimportant.*

> *Then we could look at what is on the inside of a person instead of what is on the outside. I hope my children will remain this way when it comes to learning about and interacting with other people as they grow older.*

People hearing her remarks listened hopefully. Being blind and deaf to the individual differences that should not matter in how people are viewed and treated is an idea that captures the essence of full diversity.

When organizational leaders and employees reach this point, prejudice and discrimination will be driven from the workplace and replaced by principles, genuine caring, harmonious and fulfilling relationships, and fully contributing employees.

When organizational leaders and employees reach this point, it will no longer be necessary to know a person's race, gender, or other physical, cultural, or ethnic differences before operational or employment decisions are made. Principles will drive individuals to do the right thing.

CONCLUSION

Perhaps the most important step in getting started is deciding. This decision is executed, not by straddling the fence, waiting to turn back when things get tough, but by fully and freely going forward.

All who will benefit from effective diversity management—women of all races, minority men, white men, everyone—must be both active and proactive in the quest to eradicate prejudice and discrimination.

Through perseverance, two paths converge—one formerly traveled by organizational leaders seeking breakthrough successes, the other, a parallel path along which the ideals and principles of diversity management have traveled alone. Blending these two paths will ultimately create a cultural renaissance, freeing our organizations, indeed, our larger world, from prejudice and discrimination

Dr. Martin Luther King, Jr., in his visionary wisdom, spoke of our leadership in the journey as the task of *"building a world without want, without hate, where all men and women live together in shared opportunity and brotherhood"* (King, 1964, p. 7).

As the U.S. embarks upon a world market and the 21st Century, I believe we are up to the challenge.

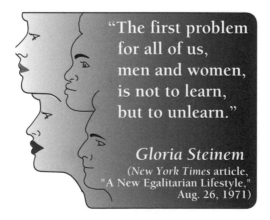

"The first problem
for all of us,
men and women,
is not to learn,
but to unlearn."

Gloria Steinem
(*New York Times* article,
"A New Egalitarian Lifestyle,"
Aug. 26, 1971)

"If you have no confidence in self you are twice defeated in the race of life. With confidence, you have won even before you have started."

Marcus Moziah Garvey
Philosophy and Opinions (1923)

EPILOGUE

Sometimes I wonder just what I'm fighting for.
I win some battles, but I always lose the war.
Hanging out there in this no man's land out there...
But I know, people I said I know,
It's just gotta be a better world somewhere."
—B.B. King

This book has described the problems of prejudice and discrimination and the often-silent havoc they wreak. Unfortunately, the enormity of the problems could leave the reader with the sense that these issues are too difficult to tackle—especially, since no one has yet seen the benefits of efforts to eliminate them.

Racism and sexism are as pervasive as ever. Indeed, they rear their ugly heads at will, almost daring people to challenge them. If past history is any indication, they will continue to enjoy a safe environment in which to freely operate.

Meanwhile, the masses will continue to sing the same old tunes:

♪ *I'm just one person; what can I do?*

♪ *You call that discrimination? Why the same thing happened to me once.*

♪ *You're just too sensitive. You are taking yourself much too seriously.*

♪ *I'm tired of you people blaming race and sex for your problems.*

♪ *This problem will certainly never go away in my lifetime.*

♪ *You can't legislate morality; people have a right to believe whatever they want.*

♪ *It's too hard to confront someone about these things.*

♪ *You can believe I'll never work for one.*

♪ *What's the problem? You people do all look alike.*

♪ *Women don't have any business trying to compete with men.*

♪ *Will things ever get any better?*

How do we shake these tired old blues?

The reader is reminded that we all have a responsibility to work toward creating the kind of environments we wish to work in just as we do the kind of world we wish to live in. When we accept that responsibility, we will quickly realize it is not just someone else's problem; it's our problem, too. It will take all of us, not just other people, to correct it

The problems of racism, sexism, prejudice, and discrimination, ultimately stem from notions of superiority and inferiority. Sociologist Gordon Allport said the easiest thing to convince someone of was his or her superiority to someone else.

We need to ask ourselves:

- Did Allport possibly mean me? Or was he just referring to other people?

- If he meant me too, what is behind my willingness to embrace notions of superiority and inferiority? Why have I consciously or subconsciously bought into stereotypes?

- Although I may have spent a lifetime embracing and acting on my stereotypical beliefs, is it too late to change?

- Finally, what's in it for me to change?

Granted, such tough self-reflection may be easier to avoid. But if we approach these questions with honesty and without denial, rationalization, and rejection, the resultant understanding and self-awareness will be gratifyingly rewarding.

As much as we might like it to, resolution will not come about on its own; we will have to initiate it. Thus, we have a unique opportunity to redefine human relationships, to ensure the greater success of our organizations, and to rewrite our nation's future for the history books.

Eradicating racism and sexism, products of centuries-old, human-relations practices, will be a tremendous challenge, but if everyone steps up to the plate, the outcome will be assured. And who ultimately stands to gain from the resolution of this massive problem? Women of all races, minority men, and white men—in other words, all of us.

B. B. King's song pleads for a better world. Yes, Mr. King, there is a better world, and it is within our reach—as close as our own minds, choices and actions. We simply must pass over that great wall of rejection, that powerful sea of rationalization, and that forbidden mountain of denial. A better world awaits us all when we finally work our way past the stumbling blocks in our organizations and ourselves.

As more and more people become prejudice-free, and companies create prejudice- and discrimination-free workplaces, there will be an amazing reformation in our work and personal lives that will allow us to shake off those *Diversity Blues* and finally start singing a different tune.

...The colors of the rainbow so pretty in the sky;
smiles on all the faces of all the people passing by.

I see friends shaking hands saying how do you do.
But what they're really saying is I love you.

I see trees of green, red roses too.
I see them bloom for me and you.

And I think to myself, what a wonderful world.

Oh yeah!

—Louis Armstrong

A full appreciation for human diversity can be reached when people no longer define (or judge) each other based on cultural or physical attributes, but on the content of their character

When organizational leaders and employees reach this point, prejudice and discrimination will be driven from the workplace and replaced by principles, genuine caring, harmonious and fulfilling relationships and fully contributing employees of productive 21st Century organizations.

GLOSSARY

Acceptance deprivation: The condition of being denied acceptance that causes a strong desire for it.

Advantaged: Being in a relatively favored position.

Affirmative-action programs: Action taken to provide equal opportunity for women and minority men and other protected classes.

Afrocentrism: Centered on Africa and other things peculiar to Africa.

Appreciating and capitalizing on human differences: Recognizing the significance and valuing the diversity among people.

Arranged mentor: An agreed to or planned relationship between a high-ranking manager and a lower-level person which aids the lower-level person in being successful in his or her career.

Assumption of sameness: Presumed uniformity between people of like race, ethnicity, gender, or any group.

Benchmarking: Measuring something against a standard, particularly a standard that surpasses all others.

Bigotry: The attitude of intolerance toward anything not of one's own group.

Capitalizing on human differences: To turn human diversity to advantage.

Civil Rights legislation: Laws prohibiting discrimination for reasons of race, gender, ethnicity, etc.

Confronting differences: Facing individual differences head on.

Coping skills: Methods that enable people to contend with negative situations.

Corporate ladder: The steps up the hierarchical path to upper management.

Covert discrimination: See "subtle discrimination."

Cross-cultural training: See "diversity training."

Cultural heritage: Characteristics, traditions and birthright of a community passed down through generations of people.

Defense strategies: See "ego defenses," "coping skills."

Dehumanize: To deprive someone of human qualities or attributes and treatment.

De-institutionalize: To disallow something as being the norm or status quo.

Demography: The characteristics and vital statistics of human populations.

Difference: The quality of being dissimilar; a disagreement or controversy.

Disadvantaged: Suffering under severe economic and social limitation.

Disciplinary action: Punishment for undesirable behavior.

Discrimination: Behavior marked by prejudice.

Discrimination-free work environment: Workplace that has successfully eliminated discrimination against any group.

Disparity: The condition of being unequal.

Diversity: The quality of being different.

Diversity training: A course that teaches awareness of racial, ethnic, and gender differences among people and issues caused by those differences.

Double standard: Permitting greater opportunity or liberty to one person or group than to another.

Ego defenses: See "coping skills."

Employee morale: The state of happiness, fulfillment, satisfaction and willingness to work among an organization's employees.

Employee productivity: The level of a work group's creation of goods and services to enhance the wealth and value of that organization.

Employee retention: The rate at which employees continue to work in an organization.

Employee utilization: Utilizing an employee's capabilities in an organization.

Empowered: To be endowed with authority and power.

Ethnic double consciousness: Facing discrimination from two standpoints, e.g. minority women who face both racial and gender discrimination.

Ethnicity: Pertaining to a particular religious, racial, national, or cultural group.

Exclusionary: Leaving out certain people or denying their rights and privileges.

Experiential training program: A program for which benefits are derived from experiencing the lessons taught.

Federal Glass Ceiling Commission: An organization within the Department of Labor that deals with the restricted upward movement for women in organizations.

Formal networking: A regular program or system that enables groups of people to be connected with one another to gain the benefit of support.

Gender differences: Differences between males and females.

Glass ceiling: The barriers that restrict the upward movement of women in organizations, often used to represent lack of upward mobility for minorities as well.

Heterogeneous: Consisting of dissimilar parts. Not homogeneous.

Homogeneous: Of the same or similar kind; uniform in composition.

Hostile work environment: A work culture marked by negativism and antagonism toward some groups.

Human differences: The gamut of distinctive qualities and attributes between people.

Human interactions: Communication and other contact and actions between people.

Human relationships: Attitude or stance that people assume toward one another. Connections and dealings among people.

Human resource acquisition: See "Recruitment."

Inclusive: Taking everything within its scope.

Informal networking: An unplanned system of connecting people with one another for the benefit of support.

Institutional: Adherence to established norms; given the characteristic of an institution.

Internalized oppression: The act of embodying negative beliefs and stereotypes about oneself.

Interpersonal feedback: Constructive information given between and about people.

Inter-racial: Involving more than one race.

Intra-gender: Within the same gender.

Intra-racial: Within the same race.

Invisible differences: Differences between people that are not immediately apparent or obvious.

Legislation-based diversity management: Managing work force differences as dictated by law.

Managing diversity: A managerial process that creates an environment that is non-hostile for all employees and in which all employees are able to contribute to their fullest.

Media: Conveyor of data to the public through newspapers, magazines, television, etc., and reaching a large audience

Mentor: A high ranking, influential organization member who is committed to providing career support to an individual.

Minority: A member of a group that is smaller in number than the larger group of which it is a part.

Mixed-race team: A group comprised of individuals of more than one race.

Multi-cultural: Related to several different cultures.

Non-white person: Any of a number of groups of people not classified as Caucasian.

Optimum work environment: A work culture that is conducive to every employee working at his or her full capacity.

Organizational culture: A work environment created by an organization's principles, norms, policies, practices, and relationships between people.

Organizational development: Growing and strengthening an organization through building skills and relationships among its employees.

Organizational effectiveness: The organization's ability to function in a way that produces the desired outcome with minimal effort.

Organizational productivity: The creation of goods and services and production of wealth and value by an organization's members.

Overt discrimination: Open and observable prejudicial actions or behavior.

Parity: Equality.

Performance ratings: An organization's method of evaluating employee performance.

Polarization: A divisive concentration of conflicting or contrasting positions.

Preferential treatment: Receiving or providing preference to one person or group over another.

Prejudge: Judging beforehand without adequate evidence.

Prejudice: A preconceived preference or idea; bias; adverse judgment without examining the facts.

Prejudice-free work environment: A work climate in which no one is treated with prejudice; a non-hostile environment.

Principle: A code of conduct that influences how people think and act.

Principle-based management practices: Managing all employees by a standard of moral or ethical behaviors.

Privileged: Having special permission, advantages, or rights.

Quota: An allotment or proportional share assigned to a group.

Racial: Of or pertaining to race

Racial inferiority: The supposed lesser degree or rank of one race when compared to another.

Racial superiority: The supposed greater degree or rank of one race when compared to another.

Racially diverse: Groups comprised of people of different races.

Racism: Discrimination or prejudice based on race.

Recruitment: The process of identifying and enrolling new members into an organization.

Reverse discrimination: Preferential treatment toward women and minority members in order to correct the wrongs of past racial and gender discrimination.

Same race teams: Teams whose members are all the same race.

Self-fulfilling prophecy: The fulfillment of expectations.

Senior manager: One of the upper-ranking members of management.

Sensitizing: Making people aware of themselves in relation to others.

Sexism: Prejudice and discrimination directed at people based on gender.

Sexual harassment: Repeated unwanted sexual advances, usually toward someone subordinate to the perpetrator.

Significant emotional event: An occurrence that engenders emotions strong enough to alter people's deeply-rooted ideas and beliefs.

Socialization: To adapt people to the norms, beliefs, values, etc. of the larger group.

Sponsor: See "mentor."

Stereotypes: Rigid beliefs about groups that are held by significant numbers of people.

Subtle discrimination: Hidden or secret prejudicial actions or behavior.

Support network: An entity through which particular groups can connect with one another to resource with and provide encouragement to each other.

Teachable moment: A development with a message so obvious, it speaks for itself, offering immediate insight to people.

Team growth: The development of a team through the improvement of relationships and the ability of its members to work together.

The Golem Effect: See "self-fulfilling prophecy."

Tokenism: Making a symbolic gesture to indicate a greater accomplishment.

Turnover: Hiring employees to replace those who have left.

Underprivileged: Applies to people who do not have the same opportunities or advantages relative to others.

Unresolved differences: Failure to bring disagreements to a successful resolution.

Value-added syndrome: A belief that certain groups bring more to the table than others.

Valuing differences: See "appreciating and capitalizing on human differences."

Visible differences: Readily apparent distinctive attributes about people.

Visible minority: A person who, based on outward appearances, is obviously a member of a minority group.

White-male norm: The lifestyle standard attributed to white males.

White-male privilege: Advantages granted to white males above other groups.

White privilege: Advantages granted to white people above other races.

Within-Group Differences: Differences that occur within homogeneous groups.

Women and minorities: The phrase commonly used to refer to women of all races and minority men.

Work force: All people working or available to work in an industry or the nation.

Work force composition: See "work force demographics."

Work force demographics: The characteristics and vital statistics of the work force.

Work force diversity: The various racial, ethnic, and gender groups that comprise the work force.

Workplace environment: See "organizational culture."

REFERENCES

Abbasi, S. M., & Hollman, K. W. (1991, July). Managing cultural diversity: The challenge of the '90's. *Records Management Quarterly, 24-32.*

Allen, G. (1991, May). Valuing cultural diversity: Industry woos a new work force. *Communication World,* 8 (6), pp. 14-17.

Allport, G. W. (1958). *The nature of prejudice.* New York: Doubleday.

American Heritage Dictionary. (1985). p. 1020. Palo Alto, CA: Houghton Mifflin.

Babad, E.Y., Inbar, J., & Rosenthal, R. (1982). Pygmalion, Galatea, and the Golem investigations of biased and unbiased teachers. *Journal of Educational Psychology, 74,* 459-474.

Barnett, M. R. (1982, February). Nostalgia as nightmare: Blacks and American popular culture. *The Crisis,* n.p.

Barnett, S. (1981, June 23). Observing an unwelcome attitude returns. *Advertising Age,* p. 48.

Barnhart, G. (1996). The inherent challenges facing white men in engaging in diversity initiatives [Unpublished manuscript].

———. (1996). Vision of a desired state re: diversity [Unpublished manuscript].

Becoming antiracist/racists. *Education & racism. An action manual.* (1973). Washington, D.C.: National Education Association.

Blank, R. & Slipp, S. (1994). *Voices of diversity: Real people talk about problems and solutions in a workplace where everyone is not alike.* New York: Amacom.

Braham, J. (1987, November 15). Is the door really open? *Industry Week,* n.p.

———. (1989, February). No, you don't manage everyone the same. *Industry Week,* pp. 28-30, 34, 36.

———-. (1989, February). No, you don't manage everyone the same. *Industry Week,* pp. 28-30, 34, 36.

Brown, J. & Batts, V. (1985). Helping blacks cope with and overcome the personal effects of racism. Paper presented at The American Psychological Association Convention, Los Angeles.

Catalyst, (1997). *Women of color in corporate management, A statistical picture.* n.p.

Caudron, S. (1993, April). Training can damage diversity efforts. *Personnel Journal,* 72 (4), 50-52.

Cincinnati flunks ABC gender test. Primetime Live. *Cincinnati Enquirer.* (1993). p. 1.

A Class Divided [Video and study guide]. (1985). Alexandria, VA: Yale University Films.

Collins, P. Hill. (1990). *Black feminist thought: Knowledge, consciousness, and the politics of empowerment.* Boston: Unwin Hyman.

Conlin, J. (1989, December). Racism at meetings. *Successful Meetings,* 38 (13), 48 - 52.

Cox, T. H. (1993). *Cultural diversity in organizations: Theory, research and practice.* San Francisco: Berrett-Koehler.

Cox, Jr. T. H., & Blake, S. (1991). Managing cultural diversity: implications for organizational competitiveness. *Academy of Management Executive,* 5, (3), 45-56.

Cox, T. H., & Harquail, C. V. (1991). Career paths and career success in the early stages of male and female MBAs. *Journal of Vocational Behavior,* 39, 54-75.

Cross, E. Y. (1992, January/ February). Making the invisible visible. *Healthcare Forum Journal,* n.p.

Cross, E. Y., Katz, J. H., Miller, F. A., & Seashore, E. W. (Eds.). (1994). *The promise of diversity: Over 40 voices discuss strategies for eliminating discrimination in organizations.* New York: Irwin Professional Publishers.

Dovido, J. F., & Gaertner, S. L. (Eds.). (1986). Prejudice, discrimination and racism. New York: Academic Press.

Elkins, S. M. (1959). *Slavery: A problem in American institutional and intellectual life.* Chicago: University of Chicago Press.

Federal Glass Ceiling Commission. (1995, March). *Good for business: Making full use of the nation's human capital.* Washington, D.C.

———. (November, 1995). *A solid investment: Making full use of the nation's human capital.* Washington, D.C.

Floyd, T. (1969). *Integration is a bitch.* Opinion News, n.p.

Flower, J. (1992, September/October). Differences make a difference. *Healthcare Forum Journal,* 62-69.

Freire, P. (1972). *Pedagogy of the oppressed.* Harmondsworth: Penguin.

Galen, M., & Palmer, A. T. (1994, January 31). White, male and worried. *Business Week,* n.p.

Gibbs, B. & Terry, R. (1977, Spring). Advocating change in the white male club. *Civil Rights Digest,* n.p.

A tale of O [film]. (1979). Cambridge, MA: Goodmeasure, Inc.

Grant, J. (1987). Women as managers: What they can offer to organizations. *Organizational Dynamics,* n.p.

Gray, W. H. (1996, May 13). [Speech]. Second National Symposium on Equity and Education Testing and Assessment. Washington, D.C.

Greenhaus, J. H., Parasuraman, S, & Wormely, W. (1990). Effects of race on organizational experiences, job performance evaluations and career outcomes. *Academy of Management Journal,* (33), 644-686.

Gregory, A. (1990). Are women different and why are women thought to be different? Theoretical and methodological perspectives. *Journal of Business Ethics,* 9, 257-266.

Griggs, L. B. & Louw, L. L. (Eds.). (1995). *Valuing Diversity: New tools for a new reality.* New York: McGraw Hill.

Hacker, A. (1992). *Two nations, black and white, separate, hostile, unequal.* New York: Scribner.

Hankins, Grover. (1997, September). The Civil Rights Act of 1991: Where do we go from here? [Speech]. Continuing Legal Education Symposium, Texas Southern University, Thurgood Marshall School of Law.

Harper, P.A. (2000, January 19). Industry gets 'C+' for minority ads. *Associated Press Online,* p. 1.

Hyman, B. (1981). *How successful women manage.* New York: American Management Association's Extension Institute.

Johnson, A. (1987, December). Black managers still have a dream. *Management Review,* pp. 20-27.

Jones, E. W. (1986, May/June). Black managers: The dream deferred. *The Harvard Business Review,* pp. 84-93.

Kanter, R. M. (1988). Ensuring minority achievement in corporations: The importance of structural theory and structural change. In Watts & Carter (Eds.). (1991, September). Psychological Aspects of Racism in Organizations. *Group & Organizational Studies,* 16 (3), n.p.

———. (1977). *Men and women of the corporation.* New York: Basic Books.

King, M. L., Jr. (1964). A mighty army of love. *SCLC Newsletter,* Vol. 2. (Oct.-Nov., 1964), p. 7.

King, C. (1981, March). White people must change. *CBS News Special Report: The Agony of Atlanta.*

King, D. K. (1988). Multiple jeopardy, multiple consciousness: The context of a black feminist ideology. *Journal of Women in Culture and Society,* 14 (1), 42-72.

Klemmerer, B. E., & Arnold, V. A. (1993, Winter/Spring). The growing use of benchmarking in managing cultural diversity, *Business Forum.* 18 (1, 2), 38-40.

Kotter, J. P. (1996). *Leading change.* Boston: Harvard Business School Press.

LaPorte, S. B. (1991, January). The sting of the subtle snub. *Working Woman,* 16 (1), pp. 53-55.

Livingston, A. (1991, January). Twelve companies that do the right thing. *Working Woman.* 16 (1), pp. 57-60.

Loftus, P. (1992, September/ October). The Pygmalion effect. *The Canadian Banker,* 99 (5), pp. 34-38.

Management Review. (April, 1993). Managing diversity for competitive advantage. p. 6.

Mann, E. (1991). L. A.'s Lethal Air. Los Angeles: *Labor Community Strategy Center Publications.* (Frederick Douglass speech to West Indian Emancipation, Aug. 4, 1857.)

Martin, L. G., & Ross-Gordon, J. M. (1990, Winter). Cultural diversity in the workplace: Managing a multicultural work force. *New Directions for Adults and Continuing Education,* no. 48, pp. 45-54.

Massey, M. (1986). *What you are is where you were when* [Film]. n.p.: Video Publishing House.

McIntosh, P. (1986, April). White privilege and male privilege [paper]. Virginia Women's Studies Association, Richmond, Virginia.

———-. (1986, October). White privilege and male privilege [paper]. The American Educational Research Association, Boston.

Moore, R. B. (1976). Racism in the English Language. New York: Racism and Sexism Resource Center for Educators.

Morrison, A. M. (1993, April). Diversity: A special report. *Training and Development,* pp. 39-43.

———. (1992). *The new leaders. Guidelines on leadership diversity in America.* San Francisco: Jossey-Bass.

Multi-Media Productions. (1981, September). *Racism* [Film]. The Phil Donahue Show.

National Public Radio Morning Edition. (1994, May 31). Cultural diversity programs.

———. (1995, August 11). Affirmative action programs.

———. (2000, February 4). On Jill Barad's departure as Mattel Company's CEO.

Nemeth, C. J. (1986). Differential contributions of majority and minority influence. *Psychological Review,* 23-32.

New York Amsterdam News. (1996, March 16). 87, (11:4), 36.

Nichols, E. (1991). The philosophical aspects of cultural diversity [Speech]. Procter & Gamble, Cincinnati.

Norment, L. (2000, January). New faces in executive suites. Ebony. (LV:3) 42-48.

Olson, C. A., & Becker, B. E. (1983). Sex discrimination in the promotion process. *Industrial and Labor Relations Review,* (36), pp. 624-641.

Olson, J. E., & Frieze, I. H. (1987). *Income determinants for women in business.*

Owens, J. V. (Aug., 1993). Women in manufacturing: Engendering change. *Cost Engineering.* 35(8), pp. 11-18.

Powell, Colin, gives opening keynote speech at GOP convention. (1996, September 2). *Jet,* 90, no.16, 14.

Ragins, B. R. (1989). Barriers to mentoring: The female manager's dilemma. *Human Relations,* 42, 1-22.

Ragins & Cotton (1991). Easier said than done: Gender differences in perceived barriers to gaining a mentor. *Academy of Management Journal.* 34 (4), 939-961.

Ramic Productions. (1987) *The Pike Syndrome* [Film].

Roberts, B.E. (1998). Roberts vs. Texaco: A true story of race and corporate America. New York: Avon.

Rollins, E. B. (1988). *Partners in Chaos: The joy, excitement, pain and danger of managing the new cultural diversity in the American workplace and society.* New York: Mountaintop Ventures, Inc.

Rosen, B. & Jerdee, T. H. (1974, March/April). Sex stereotyping in the executive suite. *Harvard Business Review,* 52 (2), 45-58.

Schreibman, T. (1996, July). The invisible woman. *New Woman,* p. 69.

Shearer, J.M. (1994). *Enter the river. Healing steps from white privilege toward racial reconciliation.* Scottdale, PA: Herald Press.

Snyder, R. A. (1993, Spring). The glass ceiling for women: Things that don't cause it and things that won't break it. *Human Resource Development Quarterly,* 4 (1), n. p.

Snyder, M. (1982, July). Self-fulfilling stereotypes. *Psychology Today, n.p.*

The Sun Newspaper [Baltimore], (1987, July 3).

Tajfel, H. (1970). Experiments in intergroup discrimination. *Scientific American,* 223, 96-102.

Thomas, K. M., & Kruh, N. (1994, February 13). Collecting controversy. *The Dallas Morning News,* n.p.

Tutu, Archbishop D. M. (1994, June 14). Racism [Address]. Cincinnati, Ohio.

United States Bureau of the Census.

United States Bureau of Labor Statistics.

York, D. E. (1994). *Cross-Cultural Training Programs*. Westport, CN: Bergin & Garvey.

Walanabe, S. (1991). The Japanese quality control circle: Why it works. *International Labour Review.* 130 (1), n.p.

Watts & Carter. (1991, September). Psychological aspects of racism in organizations. *Group & Organizational Studies,* 16 (3), n.p.

Webster's Ninth New Collegiate Dictionary. (1985). Springfield, MA: Merriam-Webster, Inc.

———. (1990) Merriam-Webster, Inc., Springfield, MA.

Winikow, L. (1991, February 1). How women and minorities are reshaping corporate America. *Vital Speeches.* 57 (8), 242-244.

York, D. E. (1994). *Cross-cultural training programs*. Westport, CN: Bergin & Garvey.

INDEX

D

E

ABOUT THE AUTHOR

Since 1975, Dr. Gladys Gossett Hankins has been a manager at The Procter & Gamble Company, one of Fortune 500's largest corporations, headquartered in Cincinnati, Ohio. In many of her positions, she has broken through barriers as the first woman manager, and the first African American. Her varied management assignments have bridged manufacturing and the corporate arena.

Dr. Hankins has been a pioneer in developing practical methodology to aid executives and groups in learning about diversity to increase their productivity. In addition, she is recognized as an expert in global diversity. For more than 20 years, she has conducted training programs within Procter and Gamble throughout the United States as well as in Europe, Japan, Canada, and Latin America. She has also consulted with several major U. S. corporations.

She is a proven leader in designing breakthrough learning initiatives such as leadership workshops, women's development programs, and "diversity dialogues" across various dimensions of difference such as race, nationality, class, gender, sexual orientation and ethnicity. She has received numerous testimonials on her personal effect and significant impact on individuals and organizations.

Dr. Hankins holds a Bachelor of Science Degree in Business Administration with a major in Industrial Relations, and an M.B.A. Degree in Management from Rockhurst College in Kansas City, Missouri where she has been an adjunct professor in the School of Business, and from which she also received the prestigious Wall Street Journal Award for graduating first in her class. She holds a Ph.D. Degree in Organizational Behavior and Development from The Union Institute in Cincinnati, Ohio.